A CATALOGUE
OF
BRITISH FAMILY HISTORIES

οἵη περ φύλλων γενέή τοίη δὲ καὶ ἀνδρῶν

A CATALOGUE OF
BRITISH FAMILY
HISTORIES

Compiled by
T. R. THOMSON
M.A., M.D., F.R.Hist.S., F.S.A.
Fellow and formerly Honorary Librarian
of the Society of Genealogists

WITH AN INTRODUCTION BY
LORD FARRER
Late President of the Society of Genealogists

With Addenda by
GEOFFREY BARROW

THE RESEARCH PUBLISHING CO.
52 Lincoln's Inn Fields · London
IN CONJUNCTION WITH
THE SOCIETY OF GENEALOGISTS
37 Harrington Gardens · London

First published 1928
Third Edition 1976
Third Edition with Addenda 1980 ✓
© The Society of Genealogists 1980
ISBN 0 7050 0097 4
✓

Printed in Great Britain for The Research
Publishing Company (Fudge & Co., Ltd.),
Sardinia House, Sardinia Street, London W.C.2
by Biddles Ltd., Martyr Road, Guildford,
Surrey, from type-setting by Cecil Woolf,
1 Mornington Place, London N.W.1.
Bound by The Burlington Press Ltd.,
Foxton, Cambridge.

Cover design by Alan Downs.

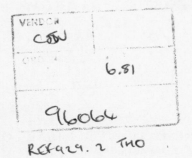

INTRODUCTION TO THE FIRST EDITION

The scope of this work has been so admirably summarised in the Preface that it only remains for me, as President of the Society of Genealogists, to welcome the publication of a book greatly calculated to assist that fascinating study. Had Pope lived today, he would perhaps have realised that his well known line,

> The proper study of Mankind is Man,

is quite inadequate. The proper study of mankind is now Man *and* Woman. The current Genealogists' Magazine laments that it is twenty years and more since Marshall published his guide, and urges that, in view of subsequent advances in the study of family history, a new edition is much needed.

Our author largely supplies this need.

Let none say that a catalogue is dryasdust. Even Charles Lamb does not reckon it among his *biblia abiblia*; he only specifies 'Court Calendars, Directories, Pocket Books, Draught Boards, bound and lettered on the back, Scientific Treatises, Almanacs, Statutes at Large; the works of Hume, Gibbon, Robertson, Beattie, Soame Jenyns; the Histories of Flavius Josephus and Paley's Moral Philosophy.'

Not a word here about catalogues.

Why, the very names of Dr Thomson's books are tempting as I turn the pages at random.

'Austen.—Chawton Manor (Hants), and its Owners.' Did the divine Jane really have ancestors?

'Barclay.—A Genealogical Account of the Barclays of Urie.' Did 'he who stood ankle deep in Lutzen's blood with the brave Augustus' brew or bank?

'Bell.—Genealogical Account of the Descendants of John of Gaunt.' Is there anyone in the London G.P.O. Directory not descended from John of Gaunt?

And so on—a feast for a 'browser'!

Let us all take to genealogy instead of cross-word puzzles, and enliven our dinner-party conversations—as the peers in a certain novel were supposed to when at a loss for congenial topics—by asking our neighbour for the Christian and surnames of his or her four great-grandfathers and four great-grandmothers.

So will the study of genealogy flourish, and perhaps (I say it with reverence) the above question will find its way (under a Labour Government, of course) into the 'curriculum' of 'elementary' if not of 'secondary' schools, when greyhound racing and the nature of 'odds' (now taught in schools as 'stocks and shares') has long been forgotten.

I welcome this useful book.

FARRER

Christmas 1927

PREFACE TO THIRD EDITION

This book purports to be a complete list of British Family Histories, that is, books written as histories of families generally acknowledged to be English, Scots, Welsh or Irish.

I have not attempted to include reprints from periodicals, mere pedigree collections, biographies, peerage claims, the publications of the Clan Societies, histories of businesses, and works published in America. Generally speaking, books in these categories, and books dealing with more than one family, are excluded.

In searching for a family history readers should not omit a search in the catalogue of the library of the Society of Genealogists. This contains many borderline works which I may not have considered to qualify for admission here. American searchers should consult the current genealogical bibliography of the Library of Congress.

As regards presentation I have given, where possible, the title, author, place and date of publication, size if not octavo, and number of copies printed if the issue was limited. An asterisk denotes 'privately printed'.

I am able to say that this book is a great improvement on the earlier editions. I have been able to introduce more entries, both old and new, and I have corrected many mistakes.

No bibliography is complete, and it will be recognised that it has been no light task to compile even the small volume now presented. A few of these books are well-known works, more are of a very limited issue, and very many, whether so stated or not, have been privately printed. Of the books themselves, some are monumental and full of the evidence of high scholarship. Thence downward there is a very varied range until the obviously unreliable (to use a mild term!) is reached.

Genealogists no longer turn to the visitations and concocted pedigrees of the earlier heralds or to a peerage or Family History as an authority, but did not the elder Pliny say that no book is ever so bad as to be absolutely good for nothing? An attentive searcher may often find grain among the chaff.

After publication I intend to make over the copyright to the Society of Genealogists who undertake the publication of the present edition. I hereby acknowledge the great help which they have given. My thanks are further offered to Mr J. S. W. Gibson, to Mrs Elizabeth McCance, to the staff of the London Library and to very many correspondents.

T. R. T.

Cricklade,
March 1975

A

Abbot—Some Records . . . of the Abbott Family . . . Thanet, by
    W. D'A. Abbot, Capetown, 1912
Family Potters, by J. P. Abbott, Kaye and Ward, 1971.

Abercromby—Genealogy of the Family of Abercromby 1456-
    1895, by The Rev. A. W. C. Hallen.
The Family of Abercromby, by C. D. Abercromby, 4to,
    Aberdeen, 1927.

Adams—A History of the Families of Adams and Peers, by The
    Rev. B. W. Adams, Calcutta, 1891.
Genealogical History of the Family of Adams of Cavan by the
    Rev. Ben. W. Adams, D.D., ed. and revised by M. W. R. P.
    Adams, 1903. (50)
A History of the Adams Family of North Staffordshire . . . ,
    by Percy W. L. Adams, 4to, St Catherine Press, 1914.
Ten Generations of a Potting Family, by Robt. Nicholls,
    London, 1930.
See also Peers.

Addington—The Annals of the Addington Family, by E. M. G.
    Belfield, Winchester, 1959.

Adeane—The Book of Dene, Deane, Adeane; a Genealogical
    History, by Mary Deane, 4to, 1899.

Adeney—The Name and Family of Adeney or Adney, by F. A.
    Allen, n.d.

9

Agnew—The Agnews of Lochnaw . . . a History of the Hereditary
Sheriffs of Galloway . . . by Sir A. Agnew, Bt., Edin., 1864;
2nd edn., 2 v., 1893.

Ainsworth—The Ainsworths of Smithills, by W. Brimelow,
Bolton, 1881.

Aislabie—A Genealogical Account of the lords of Studley Royal,
by J. R. Walbran, 1841.

Aiton, Ayton, Aytoun—The Aytons of Ayton in the Merse . . . by
Lt. Col. A. Aytoun, R.A., fo., Edin., 1887.*

Akroyd, Aykroyd—History of the Family of Akroyd in the co. of
York, comp. by F. Palliser de Costobadie, London, 1934.*

Aldersey—A Genealogical Account of the Family of Aldersey of
Aldersey and Spurstow, co. Chester, by G. C. O. Bridgeman,
4to, London, 1899.*

Alexander—Genealogical Account of the Family of Alexander, by
Ephraim Lockhart, Edin., 1836.
Memorials of the Earl of Stirling and of the House of Alexander,
by the Rev. Chas. Rogers, LL.D., 2v., Edin., 1877.

Alford—Alford Family Notes, Ancient and Modern, comp. by
Canon J. G. Alford, ed. by W. P. W. Phillimore, 4to, London,
1908.

Allnutt—The Family of Allnutt and Allnatt by A. H. Noble, 1962.

Alston—Stemmata Alstoniana, by Lionel Cresswell, 4to, 1905.

Ambler—The Ambler Family, A Record, comp. by Louis Ambler,
4to, London, 1924.

Ames—Genealogical Memoranda of the Family of Ames, by
Reginald Ames, 4to, London, 1889.*

Amory—The Descendants of Hugh Amory, 1605-1805, by G. E.
Meredith, 4to, Chiswick Press, 1901.

Amphlett—Amphlett of Clent: an Account of one of the Branches
of the Family of Amphlett in Worcestershire, by John
Amphlett of Clent, Oxford, 1908.

Anderson—The Andersons in Phingask and their Descendants, by
J. M. A. Wood, 4to, Aberdeen, 1910.
Records of a Family of Andersons of Peterhead . . . , comp. by
A. D. Ferguson and C. F. Anderson, 1936.*

Andrews—Nine Generations . . . Andrews . . . of Comber, by Sydney
Andrews, ed. by John Burls, Belfast, 1958.

Anketell, Ancketill—Memoir of the Family of Anketell, 1885.
A short History . . . of the Family of Ancketill or Anketell . . . ,
by one of its Members, Belfast, 1901.

Angus—The Angus Clan, by Angus Watson, Gateshead, 1955.

Anne—Burgh Wallis and the Anne Family, by E. M. C. Anne,
1969.

Ansell—Ansell, History of the Name, 1086-1660, by J. E. Ansell,
Adlard, 2v., 1929, 1933, (150).*

Anstruther—History of the Family of Anstruther, by A. W.
Anstruther, 4to, Blackwood, 1923.

Antrobus—Antrobus Pedigrees: the Story of a Cheshire Family,
by Sir R. L. Antrobus, 4to, Mitchell, Hughes and Clarke,
1929. (100).

Apsley—See Bathurst.

Arbuthnot—Memories of the Arbuthnots of Kincardineshire and
    Aberdeenshire, by Mrs P. S. M. Arbuthnot, London, 1920.
    (525).

Archdale—Memoirs of the Archdales, by Henry B. Archdale, 4to,
    Enniskillen, 1925.

Archer—Brief Memorials . . . of the Name of Archer, comp. by
    J. H. L. Archer, 4to, Edin., 1856;* also 4to, London, 1861.

Arden—Memoir of the Connection of Arderne, or Arden, of
    Cheshire with the Ardens of Warwickshire, by Geo. Ormerod,
    London, 1843.

Armitage—Some Account of the Family of the Armitages from
    1662 to the Present Time, by Cyrus Armitage, London,
    1850.
  The History of the Armytage or Armitage Family, by Bryan
    l'Anson, 1915.

Arnot—The House of Arnot and some of its Branches, by Jas.
    Arnot, M.D., I.M.S., 4to, Edin., 1918.

Ashburnham—History of the Family of Ashburnham, 9 pts. in
    2v., atlas fo., Pickering, 1842.

Ashe—The Ashe Family of Belfast and Trim, by the Rev. E. T.
    Martin, Dundonald, n.d.*

Askew—The Askews and Penningtons of Seaton, by the Rev. C.
    Moor, 1911.*

Aspinall—Aspinwall and Aspinall, by H. O. Aspinall, Exeter, 1923.

Atkinson—Genealogy of the Atkinsons of co. Armagh, by J. Atkinson, 1910.*

Attwood—The Attwood Family, with Historic Notes and Pedigrees, by John Robinson, Sunderland, 1903.*
The Attwood Family, by H. A. S. Attwood, 4to, paper, 1909.

Austen—Chawton Manor and Its Owners: a Family History, by W. Austen Leigh and Montague G. Knight, 4to, London, 1911.

Austin—The History of a Bedfordshire Family, by William Austin, F.S.A., Rye Hill, Luton, n.d.

Aykroyd—see Akroyd.

Ayliffe—The Ayliffes of Grittenham, Wilts, by Canon J. E. Jackson, 4to, Devizes, 1884.

Aylmer—The Aylmers of Ireland, by Sir J. Aylmer, 1931.

Ayscough—The Ayscough Family and their Connections, by J. Conway Walter, Horncastle, 1896.

Ayton, Aytoun—see Aiton.

B

Backhouse—The Descendants of John Backhouse, Yeoman, of Moss Side, near Yealand Redman, Lancashire . . . by Jos. Foster, 4to, 2v., Chiswick Press, 1894.*
Select Family Memoirs, by Jas. Backhouse, 12mo, York, 1931.*

Bagenal—Vicissitudes of an Anglo-Irish Family, by P. H. B., 4to, 1925.

Bagge—Genealogical Account of the Family of Bagge, Dublin, 1860.

Bagshawe—The Bagshawes of Ford, Derbyshire . . . , by W. H. G.
   Bagshawe, 4to, London, 1886.*

Baildon—Baildon and the Baildons; a History of a Yorkshire Manor
   and Family, by W. Paley Baildon, 4to, London, issued in 7
   parts 1912-1927.

Bailey, Baillie, Baily, Bayley—Lives of the Baillies, by Jas. Wm.
   Baillie, 4to, Edin., 1872.
   The Bailleuls of Flanders and the Bayleys of Willow Hall, by
      Francis Bayley, London, 1881.*
   The Baily Family of Thatcham . . . by L. G. H. Horton-Smith,
      Leicester, 1951.*
   The Family of Bayley of Manchester and Hope, by E. Axon,
      Manchester, 4to, 1894.

Bailey-Baker—The Families of Bailey-Baker and Baker-Gabb of
   Abergavenny, by Ric. Baker-Gabb, 4to, London, 1903.
   (50).*

Bain—The Clan Bain . . . A. I. Lawrence, 1963.

Bainbrigge—Bainbrigge Family Notes, by W. G. D. Fletcher,
   Leicester, 1890-91.

Baird—Account of the Surname of Baird, by William Baird of
   Auchmedden, ed. by W. N. Fraser, 4to, Edin., 1857; Second
   edn. of above as Dominus Fecit, Genealogical Collections
   concerning the Sir-Name of Baird; Hotten, 4to, 1870 (59).
   An appendix contains an account of the Family of Baird of
   Ordinhnivas.
   Baird of Gartsherrie; some Notices of their Origin and History
      by A(andrew) M(acGeorge), 4to, Glasgow, 1875.
   Annals of a Scots Family, by Allan F. Baird, Glasgow, 1936.*

Baker—Family Memorials . . . , relating to Baker and Conyers by
    R. G. B., 4to, 1851.

Baldwin—Some Account of the Baldwins of Ingthorpe Grange,
    Craven, Yorks, by One of Them (The Rev. J. R. Baldwin),
    Leamington Spa, 1905.

Balfour—Balfouriana Memoria, by Sir Robert Sibbald, Edin., 1699.
    The Balfours of Pilrig . . . by B. Balfour-Melville of Pilrig, 4to,
    Edin., 1907.

Ball—Ball Family Records . . . by the Rev. Wm. Ball Wright,
    Dublin, 1887; 2nd. edn., 4to, York, 1908. (250).*

Balliol—The Royal Manor of Hitchin and its Lords, Harold and
    the Balliols, by W. Wentworth Huyshe, London, 1906.
    The Norman Balliols in England, compiled in part from the
    above, with additions etc., and pedigree, by Benjamin J.
    Scott, Blades, East and Blades, 1914.
    See also Bayley.

Bankes—A Dorset Heritage, by Viola Bankes, 1953.
    The Early Records of the Bankes Family at Winstanley, by
    Joyce Bankes, Chetham Socy., 1973.

Bannerman—Some Account of the Family of Bannerman of
    Elsick, 26pp., 4to, Aberdeen, 1812.

Barber—The Barbers of the Peak, by I. J. Mitford-Barberton,
    O.U.P., 1934.

Barcham—Historical and Biographical Notices of the Barcham
    Family of Norfolk . . . comp. by Thos. Barcham, Reading,
    1857.

Barclay—A Genealogical Account of the Barclays of Urie, formerly

of Mathers, by R. Barclay, Aberdeen, 1740;* 2nd edn.,
London, 1812.

Brief Memoirs of the Barclay Family, 12mo., London, 1851.

History of the Scottish Barclays, comp. by Leslie G. de R.
Barclay, Folkestone (Bewley), 1915.

History of the Barclay Family, with full Pedigrees, by the Rev.
C. W. Barclay, 4to, St Catherine Press, 1924-25. Parts 2 and
3 comp. by Lt. Col. H. F. Barclay, St Catherine Press,
1933-4.

Barcroft—Barcroft of Barcroft, by the Rev. J. P. Barcroft, 1961.

Barker—The Barkers of Aston, by A. L. Barker, 4to, Plymouth,
1932 (125).*

Barlow—Family Records, by the Rt. Hon. Sir Montague Barlow,
Bt., and others, Derby, 1932-5.

Barnardiston—Kedington and the Barnardiston Family, by
Richard Almack, 1864.*

Barrington—The Barringtons, A Family History, by Amy Barrington, Dublin, 1917.*

Barritt—Barritts of the Fenlands, by R. A. Barritt, 1970.*

Barrow—See Pledge.

Barry—Notes on the Barry Genealogy . . . , by Sir John Wolfe
Barry, roy. 4to, London, 1906.*

Bartelot—Our Family Surname, by the Rev. R. G. Bartelot, F.S.A.,
1944.*

Bascom—See Battiscombe.

Baskerville—John Baskerville, Printer; His Ancestry by Thos. Cave, 1922 (reprinted 1936, City of Birmingham School of Printing).

Bate—Genealogies of the Families of Bate and Kirkland of Ashby-de-la-Zouche, by J. P. Rylands, 4to, 1877.

Bathurst—History of the Apsley and Bathurst Families, by Julia A. Hankey, Cirencester, 1889; 2nd edn., by A. B. Bathurst, 1902-3.

Battiscombe—A History of the Battiscombe and Bascom Families, by G. B. Barrow, 1975.

Bave—The Baves of Bath and of Barrow Court, Tickenham, co. Somerset, allied to the Harringtons both of Kelston and Corston, comp. by the Rev. F. J. Poynton, 4to, London, 1885.

Bax—The Bax Family, by Bernard Thistlethwaite, 4to, London, Headley Bros., 1936 (500).

Bayley—See Bailey.

Bayne—Historical Genealogy of Bayne of Nidderdale . . . by Joseph Lucas, Ripon, 1896 (200).

Beach—See Hicks-Beach.

Beamish—Beamish . . . co. Cork . . . by C. T. M. Beamish, Lund Humphries, 1950.

Beard—Records of a Family 1800-1933 . . . by H. McLachlan, Manchester U. Press, 1935.

Beatson—Genealogical Account of the Families of Beatson, comp.

by A. J. Beatson, Edin., 1854 (50); another edn., 4to, 1860 (70).

Beauclerk–The House of Nell Gwyn, by D. Adamson and P. B. Dewar, Kimber, 1975.

Beaufort–The Family of de Beaufort in France . . . and England, by W. M. Beaufort, 1886.

Beaufoy–Leaves from a Beech Tree, by Gwendolyn Beaufoy, Blackwell, 1930.

Beaumont–The Beaumonts in History, by Edward T. Beaumont, 4to, 1929.

Beaupré–See Bell.

Beck–The Beck Family of Northern Ireland, by John W. Beck, pamph., 1929.

Beckford–The Beckford Family; Reminiscences of Fonthill Abbey . . . , by W. Gregory, 12mo., Bath, 1887 (100);* 2nd edn., 1898 (250).

Bedingfield–The Bedingfields of Oxburgh, by K. Bedingfield, 2v., 1912-15.

Belch–The Belches of Hertfordshire, by E. and M. C. Sturge, 1929.

Belfield–The Belfield Family, comp. by H. E. Belfield, 4to, Adlard, 1930.

Bell–A Genealogical Account of the Descendants of Sir Robert Bell, With a History . . . of the Ancient Family of Beaupré, comp. by J. H. Josselyn, 4to, 1896.

Bellasis–Honourable Company . . . by Margaret Bellasis, Hollis
     and Carter, 1952/3.

Benest–A Short Account of the Descendants of Abraham Benest
     of Jersey . . . , by C. A. Bernau, 4to, pp. 10, 1906 (100).*
     Genealogical Notes on the Benests of St Helier, by C. A. Bernau,
     4to, pp. 33, 1906 (100).*

Bennett–Notes on the Ancient Cheshire Family of Bennett . . . ,
     by E. M. Hance, 1899.
     A Memoir of the Bennett Family of South Wilts., by John
     Bennett, 1952 (25).*

Benson–Genealogy of the Family of Benson of Bangor House and
     Northwoods, Ripon . . . by A. C. Benson, 4to, Eton, 1895
     (125).*

Benstede–The Benstede Family, by H. C. Andrews, roy. 4to, 1937.

Bentley–Leaves from the Past, by R. B(entley), 1896.*

Beresford–Beresford of Beresford . . . Eight Generations of a
     Gentle Family . . . , by the Revds. E. A. and W. Beresford
     and S. B. Beresford, 4to, 1893-5.*

Beresford-Hope–The Book of the Beresford-Hopes, by H. W. Law
     and Irene Law, London, 1925.

Berkeley–The Lives of the Berkeleys . . . , by John Smyth of
     Nibley (c. 1618), ed. by Sir John Mclean, 4to, 3v., Glouc-
     ester, 1883-5 (50 copies were on large paper).
     Abstracts of Smyth's 'Lives of the Berkeleys', by T. D. Fos-
     broke, 4to, London, 1820-21.
     The Berkeleys of Berkeley Square, by Bernard Falk, 1944.

Bernard–The Bernards of Abington and Nether Winchendon,

... by Mrs Nappier Higgins, 4v., 1903-4.
The Bernards of Kerry, by the Most Rev. and Rt. Hon. J. H.
    Bernard, Dublin, 1922.

Bertie—Five Generations of a Loyal House, by Lady Georgina
    Bertie, 4to, London, 1845 (Pt. I., all published).
The Albinia Book, by Mrs Wherry and A. F. Stewart, 1929
    (250).

Bethune—A Historical and Genealogical Account of the Bethunes
    of the Island of Sky, by the Rev. Thomas Whyte, Edin.,
    1778. Reprinted as a limited edition with note by A. A.
    Bethune-Baker, 4to, London, 1893.

Betts—The Betts of Wortham in Suffolk, 1480-1905, by K. F.
    Doughty, London, 1912.

Bevan—A History of the Bevan Family, by A. N. Gamble, London,
    1923-4.

Beveridge—Account of the Family of Beveridge in Dunfermline,
    by the Rev. A. W. C. Hallen, 1890.*
The Story of the Beveridge Families of England and Scotland,
    by S. A. Beveridge, 4to, Melbourne, 1923.

Bewley—The Bewleys of Cumberland, their Irish and Other Des-
    cendants, by Sir E. T. Bewley, 4to, Dublin, 1902.

Bibby—See Mellard.

Bickerton—A Concise Account of the Fall and Rise of the Family
    of the Bickertons of Maiden Castle, by John Bickerton,
    1777.

Biconylle—Excerpta Biconyllea ... by A. C. Bicknell, Taunton,
    1895 (25); revised edn., Taunton, 1900 (25).*

Biggar—The Family of Biggar, Stewartry of Kirkcudbright, 1614-1912, by G. W. Shirley, Dumfries, 1912.
See also Fleming.

Bigge—The Bigges of Lenchwick . . . , by E. A. Barnard, 1917.

Bignold—Five Generations of the Bignold Family, by Sir R. Bignold, Batsford, 1948.

Bilton—See Vipont.

Bine—See Byne.

Bingham—Memoirs of the Binghams, by Rose E. McCalmont, ed. by C. R. B. Barrett, 4to, London, 1915 (250).

Birkbeck—The Birkbecks of Westmorland and their Descendants, by Robert Birkbeck, 4to, London, 1900 (100).*

Birnie—Account of the Families of Birnie and Hamilton of Broom-hill, by John Birnie, ed. by W. B. D. Turnbull, 4to, Edin., 1838 (60).*

Biscoe—Pedigree of the Family of Biscoe, by J. C. C. Smith, 4to, London, 1887.

Bishop—A Genealogical Account of the Family of Bisshop of Bishop . . . , London, 1877.*

Bisse—Genealogical Memoranda relating to the Family of Bisse, by F. Grigson, 4to, London, 1886.

Bisset—The Old Lords of Lovat and Beaufort, by Archibald Macdonald, Inverness, 1934.

Black—A Note on the Family of Black of Over Abington 1694-

1908, with Memoranda on the Families of Willison of Red-
shaw, Steel of Annathill, and Blackie of Glasgow, 1908;
2nd edn. by W. G. Black, Glasgow, 68pp., 1924.*

Blackburne—Genealogical Memoranda relating to the Family of
Blackburne and its Alliances, comp. by the Rev. F. J. Poyn-
ton, 4to, 1874.
See also Ireland.

Blacker—A History of the Family of Blacker of Carrickblacker
. . . , by L. C. M. Blacker, Dublin, 1901.

Blackhall—The Blackhalls of that Ilk and Barra . . . , by Alex.
Morison, Aberdeen, New Spalding Club 29, 1905 (500).

Blackie—See Black.

Blackwood—The Early House of Blackwood, by Isabella C. Blackwood, Edin., pamphlet, 20pp., Edin., 1900.

Blair—Die Schottische Abstammung der Lothringer de Blair,
Hamburg, n.d.
The Family of Blair of Baltayock . . . , c. 1674 by William
Anderson, pamph., n.d. (from The Scottish Nation, 1866-7).
Five Generations of the Family of Blair, by A. T. Michell, 4to,
Exeter, 1895.

Blake—Blake Family Records, 1315—1600, by Martin J. Blake,
1st series, London, 1902; 2nd series, 1600-1700, London,
1905.
The Blakes of Rotherhithe, by Geraldine Mozley, Camelot Press,
1935.*

Blaker—Searches into the History of the Family of Blaker of
Sussex, by W. C. Renshaw, fo., London, 1894; 2nd edn.,
1904.

Blakiston—The Family of Blakiston, by H. E. D. Blakiston, O.U.P., 1928 (100).*

Bland—Collections for a History of the Ancient Family of Bland, by Nicholas Carlisle, 4to, London, 1826 (100). Index (to above) comp. by Fanny Bland, Kendal, 4to, 1890.

Bligh—The Lords of Cobham Hall, by Esmé C. Wingfield-Stratford, Cassell, 1959.

Blithe, Blyth, Blythe—A Brief Historical Sketch of the Ancient Name and Family of Blithe, Blythe, or Blyth . . . , by the Rev. William Blyth, 4to, Norwich, 1885.
Notes on the Pedigree of the Family of Blythe . . . , by E. L. I. Blyth, 4to, Edin., 1893 (100).* 2nd edn. by E. S. Blythe, 4to, Edin., 1901 (100).*

Blomfield—A Suffolk Family, by Sir Reginald Blomfield, R.A., fo., London, 1916 (100).

Blount—Collections for a History of the Ancient Family of Blount, 4to, London, 1826, (mentioned by Marshall but not traced). See also Croke.

Bloxsome—Records of the Family of Bloxsome of Gilmorton . . . , by M. Bloxsom, 1910.

Blundell—The Blundells of Bedfordshire and Northamptonshire . . . by J. H. and H. Blundell, 4to, 1912.*

Blyth, Blythe—See Blithe.

Bodington—The Bodingtons of Cubbington, by W. F. Carter, Birmingham, paper, 1896.*

Boevey—The Perverse Widow . . . , by A. W. Crawley-Boevey, 4to, 1898.

A Brief Account of the Antiquities, Family Pictures . . . for Family Use and Private Information, by A. W. Crawley-Boevey, 2v., 4to, vellum, 1912.

Bolding—Pedigree of the Bolding Family of Warwickshire, by W. B. Bickley, Birmingham, 1898;* Appendix to same, 14 pp., n.d.

Bonar—Popular Genealogists . . . , by Geo. Burnett, Edin., 1865.

Bond—Pedigree of the Family of Bond of the Isle of Purbeck, London, 1839; another edn., London, fo., 1858 (25).*

Bonham—The Bonhams of Wiltshire and Essex, by G. J. Kidston, Devizes, 1948.

Bonsor—See Hewson.

Bonville—The Story of Shute, the Bonvilles and the Poles, by Marion F. Bridie, Axminster, 1955.

Bonython—History of the Family of Bonython of Bonython, by H. F. Burke, 4to, 1901; 2nd edn., Harrison, 1926.

Boog—Traditions of the Boog Family, by C. B. Boog Watson, Perth, 1908.

Borard—The Families of Borard and Burrard, by Sidney Gerald Burrard, Dehra Dun, 1892.*

Borlase—The Descendant, Name, and Arms of Borlase of Borlase, by W. C. Borlase, London and Exeter, 4to, 1888 (200 printed, 50 of which were incomplete).

Borradaile—Sketch of the Borradailes of Cumberland, by A. F. Borradaile, 4to, London, 1881.

Borron—Borron Genealogy, comp. by J. P. Rylands, 4to, n.d.
(concerns the Borrons of Seafield Tower, Ardrossan).

Bosanquet—The Genealogy of the Family of Bosanquet, by Louisa
Clara Meyer, fo., 1877.
The Story of the Bosanquets, by G. L. Lee, Canterbury, 1966.

Bosville—The Fortunes of a Family, by Lady (A. E. B.) Macdonald
of the Isles, 2nd edn., Constable, 1928 (501).

Boswell—History . . . of the Boswells, by J. J. Boswell, folio, ? one
v. only published, London, 1906.

Boteler—Annals of the lords of Warrington, . . . by William Beaumont, 4to, 3v., 1872-3.

Botfield—Stemmata Botevilliana . . . by Beriah Botfield, Norton
Hall, 1843 (35).*
2nd edn., Stemmata Botevilliana: Memorials of the Families of
de Boteville, Thynne, and Botfield, by Beriah Botfield,
Westminster, 1858 (250).

Boughton-Leigh—Memorials of a Warwickshire Family, by B. C. F.
C. W. Boughton-Leigh, O.U.P., 1906.

Bourne—Pedigrees of the Families of Bourne; by the Rev. J.
Harvey Bloom, London, 1895 (25); 2nd edn., London,
1900 (25).*

Boutflower—The Boutflower Book . . . , by D. S. Boutflower, 4to,
Newcastle-on-Tyne, 1930.*

Bowen—The Pedigree of Bowen of Court House, comp. by Lt. Col.
E. R. Cottingham, St Catherine Press, 1927.
Bowens Court, by Elizabeth Bowen, Longman, 1942; 2nd edn.,
1965.

Bower—Notes Concerning the Bower Family of Gloucestershire, by Herbert Bower, 4to, 1871.*
History of the Bower Family, 1066-1930, by Sir Alfred Louis Bower, c. 1935.

Bowes—An Account of the Families of Boase or Bowes originally residing at Paul and Madron . . . , printed for C. W., G. C., and Fred'k Boase, 4to, Exeter, 1876 (75); 2nd edn., 4to, Truro, 1893 (100).

Bowes-Lyon—The Queen Mother's family story, by J. W. Day, 1967.

Bowker—The Bowkers of Tharfield, by I. and R. Mitford-Barberton, O. U. P., 1952.

Bowles—Records of the Bowles Family . . . by W. H. Bowles, 4to, Bemrose and Sons, 1918.*

Bowring—Benjamin Bowring and his Descendants . . . by A. C. Wardle, 1938.

Bowser—The Family of Bowser . . . by Sir Anthony Wagner, Glasgow, 1966.

Boyd—The Families of Boyds of Kilmarnock, Porterfields of Porterfield and Corbetts of Tolcross, by C. Corbett, 4to, 1816.
The Boyds of Penkill and Trochrig . . . comp. by Seymour Clarke, 4to, Edin., 1909.

Boyle—Memoirs of the Life of the . . . late Earl of Orrery and of the Family of Boyle . . . , by E. Budgell, London, 1732; 2nd edn. London, 1734; 3rd edn. 1737; 4th Dublin, 1754.
Genealogical Memoranda relating to the Family of Boyle of Limavady, by E. M. F. G. M., 4to, 1903.
Genealogical Account of the Boyles of Kelburne, Earls of

Glasgow, by hon. Robt. Boyle, 4to, Edin., 1904.*

Boynton—An Account of the Boynton Family . . . of Burton Agnes, by the Rev. C. V. Collier, Middlesborough, 1914.

Boys—Under Thirty Seven Kings, being Records of the Family of Boys, by L. B. Behrens, 4to, St Catherine Press, 1926.

Brabazon—Genealogical History of the Family of Brabazon . . . , by Hercules Sharp, 4to, Paris, 1825 (50); also 1846.
Fragment sur la maison de Barbançon en Herniault et de Brabazon en Angleterre, par M. le Chevalier de Courcelles, 4to, n.d.

Bradbrooke—The Bradbrooke Family Register, comp. by William Bradbrooke, 4to, paper, 1935.*

Brampton—Genealogy of the Brampton Family . . . by H. Hartopp, 4to, 1924.*

Branfill—Family Notes, Harrison-Branfill, by E. F. Harrison, 1873;* 2nd edn. by Col. T. A. Harrison, 1897. First Supplement (Branfill) by Col. T. A. Harrison, 1930. For Second Supplement see Harrison.

Braose—Notices of the Last of the Braose Family . . . by W. D. Cooker, London, 1856.
The Family of De Braose, 1066-1326, by D. G. C. Elwes, London, 1883.

Brett—The Brett Family, a Sketch, . . . by Frederick Brown, 1882.*

Briercliffe—The Briercliffes of Briercliffe, by R. D. and T. H. Briercliffe and E. Axon, Manchester, 1918.

Brigg—See Newsom.

Brocas—The Family of Brocas of Beaurepaire and Roche Court
. . . , by M. Burrows, London, 1886.

Brocklehurst—An Old Silk Family, 1745-1945, by Mary Crozier,
Aberdeen U. Press, 1948.*

Brockman—Records of the Brockman and Drake-Brockman Family, comp. by D. H. Drake-Brockman, 1936.*

Brodie—The Genealogy of the Brodie Family, by William Brodie,
London and Eastbourne, 1862.*
History of the Family of Brodie of Brodie, 4to, c. 1881.

Brodrick—Genealogical Memoranda relating to the Family of
Brodrick, ed. by George Harrison, 4to, 1872. (100).*
Part 2, by Viscount Midleton, 1897.

Bronte—The Brontë Family . . . , by Francis A. Leyland, 2v.,
1886.
The Brontës in Ireland, by W. Wright, 1894.

Brooke—Brooke of Horton, by K. I'Anson (G. E. Brooke),
Singapore, 1918 (100).*

Brooke-Robinson—Genealogical Memoirs of the Family of
Brooke-Robinson of Dudley, by Brooke Robinson, M.P.,
4to, Nicholls and Sons, 1896 (30).*

Brooks—Fontes . . . Brooks of Whitchurch, by the Rev. C. C.
Brooks, 1931 (30).*

Broughton—Records of an Old Cheshire Family, by Sir Delves L.
Broughton, Bt., 4to, London, 1908 (110).*

Broun, Brown, Browne—The Browns of Cultermains, Edin., 1866.
  Brown Genealogy, comp. by J. P. Rylands, 4to, 1873.
  Family Notes . . . , by Justin McCarty Brown, Hobart, 1887.
  Memorials of the Browns of Fordell, Finmont, and Vicarsgrange,
    by R. R. Stodart, Edin., 1887.
  Genealogical Memoirs of the Browne Family . . . also of the
    Peploe Family of Garnstone, by G. B. Morgan, 2 pts., 4to,
    London, 1888-91.
  The Brownes of Bechworth Castle . . . , by J. P. Yeatman, 4to,
    Lewes, 1903-4.

Brownlow—See Cust.

Bruce—Some Account of the Ancient Earldom of Carric, by
    Andrew Carrick, preface by J. Maidment, Edin., 1857 (60).
  The Bruces and the Cumyns: Family Records, by M. E.
    Cumming-Bruce, 4to, Edin., 1870.
  Notes on the Origin of the Baronial House of Bruce of
    Airth, by Maj. W. B. Armstrong, London, 1887.*
  The Bruces of Airth and their Cadets, by W. B. Armstrong, 4to,
    Edin., 1892 (105).*

Brudenell—The Brudenells of Deene, by Joan Wake, 1953; 2nd edn.,
    1954.

Brydges—Ataviae Regiae . . . by Sir Egerton Brydges, 4to,
    Florence, 1820 (60).*
  Stemmata Illustria . . . by Sir Egerton Brydges ('de Bruges'),
    fo., Paris, 1825 (100).

Brydone—Mungo Park and the Brydones of Selkirk, by J. Marr
    Brydone, London, 1963.

Buchanan—A . . . Genealogical Essay upon the Family of Buchanan,
    by W. Buchanan, 4to, Glasgow, 1723; (with the Enquiry into
    Scottish Names, 1725), Edin., 1775; Glasgow, 1793 and 1820.

The Family Book of the Buchanans of Ardoch (The Ardoch
Register), by J. P. Buchanan, Glasgow, 1894.
Strathendrick, by J. Guthrie Smith, Glasgow, 1896.

Buckler—Bucleriana . . . Notes on the Family of Buckler, by
C. A. Buckler, London, 4to, 1886.*

Buckley—A Genealogical Memoir of the Family of Buckley . . . ,
by Henry Fishwick, 4to, 1900.*

Bukenham—Notes and Extracts . . . Family of Buckenham or
Bokenham (Norfolk and Suffolk), by H. Maudslay and
W. B. Ivatts, London, 1884, Pt. I (all published) (250).*

Bullock—Memoirs of the Family of Bullock of Berkshire, Essex,
etc., by H. C. Watson Bullock, Rugby, A. J. Lawrence, 1905
(52).*

Buller—The Buller Papers (Buller of Shillingham and Morval), 4to,
1895.

Bulmer—Historical Notes on the Baronial House of . . . Bulmer,
by W. Dickon Hoyle, ed. by G. B. Bulmer, 4to, 1896.

Burdon—Records of the Family of Burdon . . . , by H. B. Tristram, 4to, 1902.*

Burman—The Warwickshire Family of Burman . . . , by R. H.
Burman, Birmingham, 1895.
The Burman Family of Warwickshire, by John B. Burman,
Birmingham, 1916.*
The Burman Chronicle, by J. Burman, Birmingham, 1940.

Burne—See Higgins.

Burns, Burnes—Notes on his Name and Family, by James

Burnes, Edin., 1851.*

Genealogical Memoirs of the Family of Robert Burns, and of the Scottish House of Burnes, by the Rev. Charles Rogers, LL.D., Edin., 1877 (also for the R. Hist. Soc.)

Burnett—Genealogical Account of the Family of Burnett of Burnetland and Barns, by Montgomery Burnett, 1845; 2nd edn. 1880.*

The Family of Burnett of Leys . . . , by George Burnett ed. by Col. James Allardyce, 4to, New Spalding Club, 1901 (525).

Burney—The House in St Martin Street, being Chronicles of the Burney Family, by C. Hill. 1907.

Burrard—See Borard.

Burrell—Burrell of Dowsby, comp. by C. W. Foster, 4to, Rotherham, 1885.

Burtt—A Lincolnshire Quaker Family 1500-1900, comp. by M. B. Burtt, Burtt Bros., Hull, 1938.

Busk—The Genealogy of the Busk Family, by Hans Busk, fo., London, 1864.

Butler—Some Account of the Family of Butler, particularly of the late Duke of Ormond . . . by — Butler, London, 1716.

A Genealogical History of the Noble and Illustrious House of the Butlers . . . London, 1771.

Genealogical Memoranda of the Butler family, by W. Butler, Sibsagor, Assam, 1845.

Butler Family History, by Patrick, Lord Dunboyne, 1966; 2nd edn. 1968.

Button—See d'Anville.

Buxton–The Buxtons of Coggleshall, by C. L. Buxton, London, Medici Society, 1910.
Belfield and the Buxtons, by G. D. Squib, 1954.*

Byles–The Byles Family, by H. N. Byles, Weymouth, 1959.*

Byne–Searches into the History of the Family of Byne or Bine of Sussex, by W. C. Renshaw, 4to, 1913 (35).*

Byres–The Families of Moir and Byres, by A. J. Mitchell Gill of Savock, 4to, Edin., 1885 (250).

Byrom–The Byroms of Manchester, by W. H. Thomson, 3v., Manchester, 1963-8 (60).

C

Cadell–The Cadells of Banton, Grange, Tranent and Cockenzie . . . , by J. H. Stevenson, fo., 1890.

Cadenhead–The Family of Cadenhead, by George Cadenhead, Aberdeen, 1887 (125).

Caillard–Family Reminiscences, by E. M. Caillard, 1887; ? a second edition, 1904.

Caird–A History of, or Note upon, the Family of Caird in Scotland, by Rennie A. Caird, 1913.

Cairncross–History of a Forfarshire Family . . . , by A. F. Cairncross, Broughty Ferry, 1920.

Cairnes–History of the Family of Cairnes or Cairns . . . , by H. C. Lawler, 4to, London, 1906 (also an edn. de luxe of 40).

Calderwood–The Calderwood Families . . . , by A. A. Taylor,

London, 1964.

Call—The Calls of Norfolk and Suffolk . . . , by Charles S. Romanes, 4to, London, 1920 (300).*

Calthorpe—Notes on the Families of Calthorpe and Calthrop . . . , comp. by Col. C. W. Carr-Calthrop, Chiswick Press, 1905; another edn., 1933.

Camac—Memoirs of the Camacs of Co. Devon, ed. by Frank Owen Fisher, 4to, Norwich, 1897 (50).*

Cambray—The Cambray Family . . . , by the Rev. J. A. Dunbar-Dunbar, 4to, London, 1898 (100).*

Cameron—History of the Camerons . . . , by Alex. Mackenzie, Inverness, 1884; also a 4to issue (75).
The Clan Cameron, by John Cameron, Kirkintilloch, 1894.
Clan Cameron, a Patriarchy Beset, by C. I. Fraser, Edin., 1953.

Campbell—A Quaint Account of the Campbells of Glenorchy, comp. by William Bowie, 1598.
The Black Book of Taymouth, ed. by Cosmo Innes, 4to, Bannatyne Club, 1855 (100).
The Book of the Thanes of Cawdor . . . , by Cosmo Innes, 4to, Spalding Club, 1859.
The MacCullum More, a History of the Argyll Family, by the Rev. Hely Smith, London, 1871.
Campbell of Kiltearn, by the Rev. Duncan MacGregor, Edin., 1874.
The Lairds of Glenlyon, by Duncan Campbell, 4to, Perth, 1886.*
The Book of Garth and Fortingall, by Duncan Campbell, Inverness, 1888.
A Memorial History of the Campbells of Melfort . . . by M. O. Campbell, 4to, London, 1882; supplement, 1894.
The Clan Campbell: Extracts from the Collections of Sir

Duncan Campbell of Barcaldine Bt., by the Rev. Henry
Paton, 4to, 8v., Edin., 1913-22.
The Story of the Campbells of Kinloch, by E. D. Login, John
Murray, 1924.
Campbell: a Family Chronicle, by Mary Campbell, Edin., 1925.*
The Book of Barcaldine, by A. Campbell Fraser, London, 1936.
The Web of Fortune, by Gwladys Campbell, Spearman, 1965.

Campbell-Maclachlan—Memorial History of the Family of Campbell-Maclachlan, by A. N. Campbell-Maclachlan, London,
1883.

Canning—Memorials of the Canynges Family . . . , by George Price,
Bristol, 1854.

Capell—Hadham Hall . . . , by W. Minet, 4to, 1914.

Carew—The Carews of Antony . . . , by Frank Halliday, David and
Charles, 1967.

Carey—The History of the Careys of Guernsey, by W. W. and E. F.
Carey, and S. C. Curtis, 4to, 1938.*

Carington—Early Records of the Smith-Carington Family . . . by
R. Smith-Carington, 4to, 1900.
History and Records of the Smith-Carington Family from the
Conquest . . . , ed. by W. A. Copinger, 2v., fo., 1907.
A Short History and Pedigree of the Carington Family . . . ,
by Arthur Carington, 4to, 1908.
See also The Great Carington Imposture, by J. H. Round in
'Peerage and Pedigree 2'; also Smith of Nottingham.

Carless, Carles—Notes to the Pedigree of Carless or Carles, by
T. A. C. Attwood, 4to, London, 1916.

Carleton—Memorials of the Carletons . . . , by Capt. P. A. Carleton,

4to, 1869.*

Carlisle—Collections for a History of the Ancient Family of Car-
lisle, by Nicholas Carlisle, 4to, London, 1822 (100).*
History of the Carlisle Family (Paisley Branch), by J. W.
Carlisle, Winchester, 1909 (100).*

Carnac—See Rivett-Carnac.

Carnegie—History of the Carnegies, Earls of Southesk, and their
Kindred, by William Fraser, 4to, 2v., Edin., 1867.*

Carr, Carre—The Family of Carre of Sleaford . . . by M. P. Moore,
Sleaford, 1863.
The History of the Family of Carr of Dunston Hill . . . Carr of
Woodhall . . . , by Col. R. E. and C. E. Carr, 4to, 3v., 1893-9;
also an extra illustrated edn., 3v., fo.

Carruthers—Records of the Carruthers Family, comp. by A. Stanley
Carruthers, 1925; revd. edn., Elliot Stock, 1934.

Carteret—A History of the Noble Family of Carteret . . . , by
Arthur Collins, 1756.

Carus-Wilson—Genealogical Memoirs of the Carus-Wilson Family
. . . , ed. by H. Carus-Wilson and H. I. Talboys, Hove, 1899
(100).*

Cary—Record of the Family of Cary, Viscount Falkland, by C. V.
Robinson, Westminster, 1864.

Cassels—Records of the Family of Cassels . . . , by Robert Cassells,
4to, 1870 (75).

Cassie—The Cassies, by R. L. Cassie, Banff, 1932.

Caunter—Caunter Family Records, by F. L. Caunter, 1930.*

Cave—The Caves of York, by T. P. Cooper, 1934.

Cavendish—Memoir of the Family of Cavendish, by White Kennett,
      D.D., London, 1708; another edn. ed. by J. Nichols, 1797.
      (The first sometimes appended to his Sermon preached after
      the funeral of William, Duke of Devonshire, 4to, ? 1732).
    The Lives of all the Earls and Dukes of Devonshire . . . , by
      Joseph Grove, London, 1764.
    The Cavendish Family, by Francis Bickley, London, 1911.

Cecil—The Life of Cecil, Lord Burghley, with Memoirs of the
      Family of Cecil, by A. Collins, London, 1732.
    The Genealogy and the Arms of the Cecils, by A. C. Fox-
      Davies, Historical Monograph Series, 1904.
    The House of Cecil, by G. R. Dennis, 1914.
    The Cecils, by Ewan Butler, Muller, 1964.
    Family and Fortune, by Lawrence Stone, O.U.P., 1973.
    The Cecils of Hatfield House, by David Cecil, Constable,
      1973.

Chadwick—A Genealogical Account of the Families of Chadwick
      of Chadwick . . . , ed. by Joseph Howard, 4to, Manchester,
      1840.

Chamberlain—Notes on the Families of Chamberlain and Harben,
      by the Rt. Hon. A. Chamberlain, Constable, 1915 (50).*

Chance—Chance of Bromsgrove and Birmingham, by J. F. Chance,
      4to, London, 1892 (50).*

Chaplin—A Short Account of the Families of Chaplin and Skinner
      . . . , by N. Chaplin, 4to, London, 1902 (50).*

Chapman—The History of the Chapman Family, by Bryan I'Anson, vol. I, 4to, 1917.*

A History of the Chapman Family, by J. P. Rylands and J. C. Mee, 1913.

Mrs Chapman's Portrait (an Account of the Chapmans of Bath), by Ruth Young, Bath, 1926.

Memoirs of my Family, by E. N. Chapman, 1928.*

Charrington–The Charrington Family, by Sir John Charrington, 1963.*

Charteris–A Family Record, by Mary wife of the 11th Earl of Wemyss, 1932.*

The Family of Charteris of Amisfield, by R. C. Reid, Dumfries, 1938.

Chase–The Chase Family of England, America, Australia, West Indies and South Africa, by A. H. Noble, 1967.

Chatburn–Carpe Diem . . . , by R. C. Chatburn, 1968.

Chatterton–New Facts relating to the Chatterton Family, by William George, 4to, 1883.

Chauncy–Pedigree of the Family of Chauncy, by Stephen Tucker, 1864: privately re-printed with additions, 4to, Mitchell and Hughes, 1884 (200).

Chester–Genealogical Memoirs of the Extinct Family of Chester of Chicheley, their Ancestors and Descendants, by R. E. Chester Waters, 2v., 4to, London, 1878-81.

Genealogical Notes of the Families of Chester of Blaby . . . by R. E. Chester Waters, Leicester, 1886.

Chetwode–Pedigree of the Family of Chetwode . . . , by Stephen Tucker, 4to, Mitchell and Hughes, 1884 (50).*

Chetwynd–The Chetwyndes of Ingestre . . . , by H. E. Chetwynd-Stapleton, Longmans Green, 1892.

Cheyne–The Cheyne Family in Scotland, by Lt. Col. A. Y. Cheyne, Eastbourne, 1931.
Cheynes of Inverugie, Esslemont and Arnage, by W. D. Cheyne-Macpherson, Kirkwall, 1943.

Chicheley–Stemmata Chicheleana . . . , ed. by Benjamin Buckler, fo. and 4to, Oxford, 1765; supplement to same, 4to, 1775 (issued together as 2v. in I. 4to.)
See also Plowden.

Chichester–History of the Family of Chichester A.D. 1086-1870 . . . , by Sir A. P. B. Chichester Bt., 4to, London, 1871.*

Child–Some Account of the Child Family 1550-1861, by Kenneth Child, Phillimore, 1973.

Chisholm–History of the Chisholms . . . , by A. Mackenzie, Inverness, 1891; also a 4to edn (75).
The Clan Chisholm, by Jean Dunlop, Edin., 1953.

Chittick–A Record of the Family and Lineage of W. G. Chittick, (Erminda Rintoul), Belfast, 1890.

Choke, Chokke–Genealogical Notes respecting the Choke or Chokke Family of Avington, Berks., by Frederick Brown, Newbury, 1882.

Cholmley–Memoirs of Sir Hugh Cholmley with some Account of his Family, written c. 1656, by Sir H. C., 4to, 1787; 2nd edn. with pedigree, 1870.*

Chorley–The Chorleys of Chorley Hall . . . , by J. Wilson, Manchester, 1907.

Christie—Genealogical Memoir of the Scottish House of Christie
. . . , by the Rev. Charles Rogers (for Royal Hist. Soc.),
London, 1878.

Christopher—The Family of Christopher . . . , ed. by A. C. Seton
Christopher, Exeter, Pollard, 1931.*

Churchill—Churchill Annals, 12mo, paper, 17–.
The Early Churchills, by A. L. Rowse, 1956.
The Later Churchills, by A. L. Rowse, 1958 (abridged edn. 1966).

Clark, Clarke—Some Account of the Clark Family . . . Middle-
ham Hall . . . , ed. by G. W. and H. H. G. Clark, 4to,
Michell Hughes and Clarke, c. 1926.*
A History of the Clarke Family . . . , by H. S. Stanley Clarke,
Ryde, Moody and Co., 1963 (75).*
See also Gordon-Clark.

Clayton—Memorials of the Clayton Family, with unpublished correspondence of the Countess of Huntingdon . . . , by the Rev.
T. W. Aveling, London, 1867.

Cleland—The Ancient Family of Cleland, comp. by J. B. Cleland,
London, 1905.

Clifford—Collectanea Cliffordiana, by A. Clifford, 3pts., Paris, 1817.*
Cliffordiana: an Account of the Cliffords of Chudleigh, ed. by
the Rev. G. Oliver, 12mo., Exeter, 1827 (?10).

Clinton—Memoirs of the Clinton Family, by Henry Fynes-Clinton,
4to, London, c. 1840.
See also Fynes-Clinton.

Clitherow—Boston Manor and the Clitherow Family, by A. J. Howard,
1969 (12).*

Clutterbuck—Collections Relating to the Family of Clutterbuck,
comp. by the Rev. R. H. Clutterbuck, Pt. I., 48pp., Stroud,

1894.

An Account of the Principal Branch of the Family of Clutterbuck . . . , ed. from the Collections of R. H. Clutterbuck,
T. W. Caltell and W. P. W. Phillimore, by M. E. N. Witchell
and C. Roy Huddleston, Gloucester, Bellows, 1924.*

Cockayne—Cockayne Memoranda . . . , by A. E. Cockayne, 2v.,
Congleton, 1869-75 (100).*

Cockburn—The House of Cockburn of that Ilk . . . , by T. H. Cockburn Hood, 4to, Edin., 1888.*

The Records of the Cockburn Family . . . , by Sir Robert
Cockburn and Henry A. Cockburn, 4to, Edin., 1913 (10
copies buckram) (250).*

Cocks—Eastnor, by the Rev. H. L. Somers-Cocks, Hereford, 1923.

A History of the Cocks Family, by J. V. Somers-Cocks,
Newton Abbott, 4pts, 1966-7.

Coke—Coke of Trunsley . . . a Family History, comp. by John
Talbot Coke, 4to, London, 1880.*

Chief Justice Coke, his Family and Descendants at Holkham,
by C. W. James, Country Life, 1929.

Colby—Some Account of the Family of Colby of Great Torrington,
Devon, by F. T. Colby, 4to, Exeter, n.d.; 2nd edn., Exeter,
4to, 1878; appendix to same 4to, 1880; 2nd appendix,
4to, 1894.

Cole—The Genealogy of the Family of Cole . . . , by J. Edwin
Cole, London, 1867.*

The Genealogie or Pedigree of Sir William Cole of the Castle
of Enniskellin . . . , by Sir W. Segar, ed. by W. Penson,
4to, 1870.

A History of the Descendants of Maximilian Cole of Oxford
. . . comp. by E. A. Loftus, 4to, Adlard, 1938.

The Cole Family of West Carbery, by the Rev. R. L. Cole, 1943.

Coleridge–The Story of a Devonshire House, by John, Lord Coleridge, London, 1905; 2nd edn. 1906.

Colley–The Family of Colley of Churton Heath . . . , comp. by T. H. Davies Colley, ed. by W. F. Irvine, 4to, Ballantyne Press, 1931 (60).

Collier–Memoirs of the . . . Rev. Arthur Collier with some Account of his Family, by Robert Benson, London, 1837.

Collins–The Family of Collins of Knaresborough, by Francis Collins, M.D., Leeds, 1912.*
The House of Collins, by D. Keir, 1952.

Colman–Memories of the Colman Family . . . , by R. B. Peake, 2v., London, 1841.

Colquhoun–The Chiefs of Colquhoun and their Country, by Sir W. Fraser, 4to, 2v., 1869 (150).*

Colt–Genealogical Memoirs of the Families of Colt and Coutts, by the Rev. Charles Rogers, Cottonian Soc. and Roy. Hist. Soc., 1879.
History and Genealogy of the Colts of that Ilk . . . , by G. F. Russell Colt, 4to, Edin., 1887 (100).*

Colville–History of the Colville Family . . . , by Sir C., C. R., and Z. Colville, 4to, Edin., 1896 (50).
The Ancestry of Lord Colville of Kinross, by G. M. Colville, London, 1887.

Comberbach–Collections for a Genealogical Account of the Family of Comberbach, by G. W. Marshall, London, 1866.*

Compton—The Descent of Charlotte Compton, Baroness Ferrers
de Chartley, by J. G. C. Clifford, 4to, London, 1892.
The Comptons of Compton Wynyates, by W. B. Compton, 1930 (200).

Constable—The Constable Family, by a member of the Evering-
ham Branch (? Thomas Angus Constable) 30pp., printed at
Market Weighton, n.d.

Conway—The Conways, by J. Evans, 1966.

Conyers—See Baker.

Cookson—Cookson of Penrith, Cumberland, and Newcastle-upon-
Tyne, by W. P. Hedley, Titus Wilson and Son, 1968.

Coote—Historical and Genealogical Record of the Coote Family, by
the Rev. A. de Vliegar, 4to, Lausanne, 1900 (there was a
special issue with 31 additional coats of arms).

Cope—Memoir of the Copes of Wiltshire, by J. C. Biddle-Cope,
4to, 1881.

Coppinger—History of the Copingers or Coppingers . . . , by W. A. Copinger, Manchester, 1882; 2nd edn., Manchester, 1884 (150).

Coppyn—The Coppyns of Kent 1300-1800, by J. M. Coppyn,
Leadenhall Press, 1900.

Corbet—The Family of Corbet, its Life and Times, by Mrs A. E.
Corbet, 4to, London, v. 1, down to 1850, 1914-17; v. 2,
1920.

Corbould—The Corbould Genealogy, by G. C. B. Poulter, Suffolk
Inst. of Archaeology, 4to, 1935.

Cornish—Cornyshe of Thurlestone. Notes to Accompany a Pedigree

of the Family, by J. T. du Boulay, 4to, Winchester, 1903.
A Family of Devon, by Vaughan Cornish, St Leonards-on-Sea,
   1942-3.

Cornwall—Genealogy of the Family of Cornwall of Bonhard, co.
   Linlithgow, comp. by R. R. Stodart, Edin., 1877.*
The House of Cornwall, by the Earl of Liverpool and Comp-
   ton Reade, 4to, Hereford, 1908.

Corrie, Corry—Records of the Corrie Family 802-1899, by J. E.
   Corrie, 4to, 2v., London, 1899.*
History of the Corry Family of Castlecoole, by the Earl of
   Belmore, London, 1891.

Costobadie—History of the Ancient Huguenot Family of Costobadie (of West Barton, co. York), by F. P. de Costobadie,
   Westminster Press, 1932 (200).*

Cotesworth—Records of the Cotesworth of Egglesburne, by
   L. E. Cotesword, n.d.*

Cottle—A History of the Cotel, Cottell, or Cottle Family, by
   W. H. Cottell, London, 1871.

Coulthart—A Genealogical . . . Account of the Coultharts of Coulthart and Collyn . . . , by G. P. Knowles, vellum, 1955 (75).*
Popular Genealogists . . . by George Burnett, Edin., 1865 (see
   also 'The Ancestor' 4. 61-80).

Couper—An Account of the Couper or Cooper Family of Scotland, by D. A. Tod, 1924.

Courson—La Maison de Courson en Bretagne et Angleterre . . .
   4to, 1881 (200).*

Courtauld—Some Earlier History of the Family of Courtauld . . . ,
   ? by G. P. Courtauld, Cassell, 1911.

Courtenay—Discours sur la Généalogie et Maison de Courtenay,

Paris, 1603.

De Stirpe et Origine Domus de Courtenay, Paris, 1607.

Histoire Généalogique de la Maison de Courtenay, par Jean du Bouchot, fo., 1661.

A Genealogical History . . . of the Family of Courtenay, by the Rev. E. Cleaveland, fo., Exeter, 1735.

The Courtenay Family, by Sir Christopher Courtenay, 1967.*

See also Tracy.

Coutts—Coutts and Co., Bankers . . . Memoirs of a Distinguished Family, by Ralph Richardson, 1901.

See also Colt.

Coventry—See Darby-Coventry.

Covert—The Coverts, by J. H. Cooper, 3pts., c. 1930.

Cowan—Alexander Cowan, his Kinsfolk and Connections, by C. B. Boog Watson, 1915,* appendix 1917.

Cowen—See Trimble.

Cox—Particulars of the Ancestry of Cox of Dunmanway, Bt., co. Cork, Book No. I, 1912.

The Cox Family of Normanton-on-Stour . . . , by G. Lissant, 1914.

Craggs—See Eliot.

Crane—Memorials of the Cranes of Chilton, by W. S. Appleton, 1868.

Craven, Cravie—Notes on the Pedigree of the Cravens of Appletree-wick, by W. J. Stavert, Skipton, 1894.

Genealogical Collections relating to the Family of Cravie or Craven in Scotland . . . , by J. B. Craven, Kirkwall, 1910.*

Crawley—History of a Bedfordshire Family, by William Austin, London, 1911.
See also Boevey.

Crawshay—The Crawshays of Cyfarthfa Castle . . . , by Margaret S. Taylor, Hale, 1967.

Cresswell—The Web of Fortune, by Gwladys Campbell, Spearman, 1965.

Crichton—Sanquhar and the Crichtons, by Douglas Crichton, Dumfries, 38pp., 1907.
Genealogy of the Earls of Erne, by the Rev. J. H. Steele, 4to, Edin., 1910 (60).*

Crispe—Collections relating to the Family of Crispe, by F. A. Crispe, fo., 4v., 1882-97 (150, but only 50 of v. 4); 5th v., i.e. New Series v. 1, roy 4to, London, 1913.

Crispin—The Crispins and Kingston-on-Hull, by M. Jackson Crispin, 1928.

Croft—Notices of the Ancient Family of Croft, by N. Carlisle, London, 1841.
The House of Croft of Croft Castle, by O. G. S. Croft, Hereford, 1949.

Crofton—Crofton Memoirs . . . , by Henry Thomas Croft and others, York, 1911.

Croke—The Genealogical History of the Croke Family originally named Le Blount, by Sir A. Croke, 4to, 2v., Oxford, 1823.*

Cromwell—Memoirs of the Protectoral House of Cromwell . . . by the Rev. Mark Noble, 2v., 1784, 2nd edn., 2v., Birmingham, 1787, 3rd edn., 2v., London and Birmingham, 1787. (A

Review of the same, by W. Richards, Lynn, 1787.)
A Short Genealogical View of the Family of Oliver Cromwell
. . . , by R. Gough, 4to, pamph., 1785.
The House of Cromwell . . . , by J. Waylen, London, 1880;
another edn. 1891; 2nd edn., ed. by J. G. Cromwell, 1897.

Cronk–An Uncommon Name . . . , Cronk Family of West Kent,
by Anthony Cronk, 1953.

Cronshaw–Some Notes on Cronshaws of Lancashire . . . , by C. H.
Denham, ed. by E. Phelps, Dublin, 1934.

Croslegh–Descent and Alliances of Croslegh . . . , comp. by Charles
Croslegh, D.D., de la More Press, 1904.*

Cross–A Family History by Richard, Viscount Cross, London, 1900.*

Crowley–Men of Iron: The History of the Crowley Family . . . ,
by M. W. Flinn.

Cruttwell–The History of the Cruttwell Family of Wokingham,
Berks., and Bath, by H. A. Cruttwell, M.D., c. 1935.

Crozier–Memorials of the Family of Crozier, by F. H. Crozier,
4to, Lymington, 1881.

Cudworth–The Cudworth Family, by J. J. Green, 4to, London,
1898.

Cullum–Genealogical Notes relating to the Family of Cullum, by
G. G. Milnes-Gibson-Cullum, 4to, London, 1928.

Cumming–The Cummings of Culter, 'Misc. Broadsides chiefly
Scottish' vol. I., three items, B.M. pressmark 1891 c.3.

Cumyn–See Bruce.

Cunliffe–Descendants of . . . the Cunliffes of Wycoller, by C. H. Owen, London, 1871; 2nd edn., 1887.

Cunningham–See Lenox-Cunningham.

Curling–Memorial Records of the Curlings of the Isles of Thanet, collected by Robert Curling, London, 1886.*

Curwen–History of the Ancient House of Curwen, by John F. Curwen, Kendal, 1928.

Curzon–See Courson.

Cust–Records of the Cust Family . . . , by Lady Elizabeth Cust, 4to, 2v., London, 1894-8; series 2, 1909, deals with the Brownlows of Belton, series 3, by Sir John Cust Bt., 1927, is biographical.
Some account of the Cust Family from the time of Edward IV . . . , by Caroline Cust, limp-boards, 1923.

D

Dallas–History of the Family of Dallas . . . , by James Dallas, ed. by C. S. Romanes, 4to, Edin., 1921.*

Dalmahoy–The Family of Dalmahoy of Dalmahoy . . . , by Thomas Falconer, 53pp., Aberdeen, 1868; 2nd edn., 1870.

Dalrymple–The Dalrymples of Langlands, by John Shaw, Bath, 1868.*
Genealogical Account of the Dalrymples of Stair, by the hon. Hew Hamilton Dalrymple, 1909.

Danvers–Memorials of the Danvers Family of Dauntsey and Culworth . . . , by F. N. Macnamara, London, 1895.*

D'Anville–Collections relating to the Families of D'anville . . . and le Grand alias Button, by 'Alton' (i.e. T. C. Button), 4to,

London, 1888 (105).

Darby–The Darbys of Coalbrookdale, by Barrie Trinder, Phillimore, 1973.

Darby-Coventry–The Family of Darby-Coventry of Greenlands, Henley-on-Thames . . . , by S. Gregson Fell, London, 1892.*

D'Arcy–Ancestral Voices, by Berta Ruck, Hutchinson, 1972.

Dasent–A West Indian Planters Family, its Rise and Fall, by Sir John R. Dasent, 1914 (25).*

Dashwood–The Oxfordshire Dashwoods, by James Townsend, Oxford, 1922.*

Daunt–Some Account of the Family of Daunt, by John Daunt, Newcastle, ? 1875 and 1881.

Davenport–William Davenport of Reading (ob. 1723) and his Descendants, by the Rev. James Davenport, 1891.*
The Davenport Family of Reading and Welford-on-Avon, by James Davenport, Worcester, 1923.
The Early History of the Davenports of Davenport, by T. P. Highet.

Davidson–The Ancestry of Randall Thomas Davidson, D.D. . . . (Davidson of Muirhouse), by the Rev. Adam Philip, London, 1903.

Davies–Genealogical History of the House of Gwysaney, by J. B. Burke, fo., London, 1847.*
Gwysaney and Owston, by G. A. Usher, Denbigh, 1964.

Dawson–The History of the Dawson Family of Farlington and

North Feriby, York . . . , by P. H. Ditchfield, London, Geo. Allen & Co., 191—.

Dayrell—The History of the Dayrells of Lillingstone Dayrell, by Eleanora Dayrell, Jersey, 1885.

Deacon—Records of the Family of Deacon of Kettering and London, by C. A. Deacon, Mitchell, Hughes, 1899.

Deane—See Adeane.

Dearman—See Atkinson.

De Beaufort—The Family of de Beaufort in France, Holland, Germany and England, by W. M. Beaufort, London, 1886.*

Debenham—A Record of the Family of Debenham of Suffolk, comp. by W. Debenham-Sweeting, St Catherine Press, 1909.*
Seven Centuries of Debenhams, by Frank Debenham, Heffer, 4to, Glasgow, 1957/8.

De Guerin—Huguenot Guerins and their Descendants . . . , by W. C. L. Guerin, London, 1873.
Kith and Kin . . . , by W. C. L. Guerin, Guernsey, 1887.
Our Kin . . . , by W. C. L. Guerin, Guernsey, 1890.*

De Havilland—A Chronicle of the Ancient and Noble Norman Family of de Havilland . . . , by Lt. Col. T. F. de Havilland, fo., Guernsey, 1852; another edn. ed. by J. Von S. de Havilland, York Herald, fo., pp. 122, 1865.

De La Touche—Genealogy of the De La Touche Family seated in France and Ireland, by Sir A. B. Stransham, 4to, 1882 (22).*

Delaval—The Gay Delavals, by F. Askham, Cape, 1955.
Those Delavals, by Roger Burgess, Newcastle, 1972.

Delves–See Broughton.

Dennistoun–Some Account of the Family of Dennistoun of Colgrain, 4to, Dumbarton, 1859; 2nd edn. by James W. Dennistoun, Glasgow, 1906.
The Dennistouns of Dennistoun, by T. F. Donald, Glasgow, 1918.

Denny–A Brief Account of the Denny Family, by A. Denny, 1883.
History of the Denny Family of Tralee, by H. L. L. Denny, 1911.

Dering–Genealogical Memoranda, relating to the Family of Dering of Surrenden Dering, by the Rev. F. Haslewood, London, 1876.*

De Trafford–History of the de Traffords of Trafford, by W. S. G. Richards, fo., 1896 (25).

De Vere–Some Account of the Family of De Vere, the Earls of Oxford, and of Hedingham Castle . . . , by the Rev. S. A. Majendie, 4to, Castle Hedingham, 1904.

Devereux–An Account of the Anglo-Norman Family of Devereux of Balmagir, co. Wexford, by G. O'C. Redmond, 4to, Dublin, 1891.

Dewar–The Dewars, formerly of King's Park and Craigniven, by P. de V. Beauclerk-Dewar, London, 1966.*

De Wasteney–Some Account of Colton and of the De Wasteney's Family, by the Rector (The Rev. Fred. P. Parker), Birmingham, 1879.*

D'Eyncourt–See Tennyson-D'Eyncourt.

Digby–My Ancestors, being the History of the Digby and

Strutt Families, by Letice Digby, 4to, London, 1928.*

Dighton—The Dightons of Clifford Chambers . . . , by Conway Dighton, 4to, London, 1902.

Dingwall-Fordyce—Family Record of Dingwall-Fordyce in Aberdeenshire . . . , by Alexander Dingwall Fordyce, 2v., Toronto, 1885-8.

Ditchfield—Memorials of the Ditchfield Family of West Loughton, by R. Walmsley, 1941.*

Dodderidge—The Dodderidges of Devon . . . , by the Rev. S. E. Dodderidge and H. G. H. Shaddick, Exeter, 1909.

Don—Memoirs of the Don Family in Angus, by W. G. Don, London, 1897.*

Done—See Egerton.

Doone—The Doones of Exmoor, by Edwin John Rawle, London, 1903.
  The Story of the Doones in Fact, Fiction, and Photo, by L. B. Thornycroft, Taunton, 1939.

Douglas—The History and Race of Douglas and Angus . . . , by David Hume of Godscroft, fo., Edin., 1644, 1648, 1657, 12mo, 2v., 1743; 8vo, 2v., 1748; other edns., Glasgow, 1814; Aberdeen, 1820; and London, 1820.
  A Synopsis of the Genealogy . . . Brigantes, or Douglas, or Angus . . . , by Pedro Pineda, text in English and Spanish, London, 1754.*
  History of the Family of Douglas of Tilwhilly or Tilliquhillie, Bath, 1874.
  The Douglas Book, by Sir William Fraser, 4to, 4v., Edin., 1885-6.

The Genealogy of the Families of Douglas of Mulderg and Robertson of Kindeace . . . , by the Rev. Gustavus Aird, D.D., Dingwall, 1895.

A History of the House of Douglas from the Earliest Times . . . , by Sir Herbert Maxwell, 2v., London, 1902(and a large paper 4to, edn., 150).

A History of the Douglas Family of Morton in Nithsdale and Fingland, and their Descendants, by Percy W. L. Adams, thick 4to, Bedford, 1921.

Douglas and the Douglas Family, by Charles C. Riach, Hamilton, 1927.

Dove–History of the Dove Family, by W. H. Hudlestone, Newcastle, 1910.

D'Oyly–History of the House of D'Oyly, by W. D. D'Oyly Bayley, 2 pts, London, 1845-57.

Drage–The Drages of Hatfield, by C. Drage, Hatfield, 1969.

Drake–Life of . . . Sir Francis Drake . . . with the Historical and Genealogical Account . . . by J. Campbell, ed. by Sir T. T. Drake, 83pp., London, 1828.

The Family and Heirs of Sir Francis Drake, by Lady Eliott-Drake, 2v., 1911.

Drake-Brockman–See Brockman.

Drayton–See Alno.

Driffield–History of the Driffield Family from 1537 to 1902, by E. B. Driffield, Liverpool, 1907.*

Drinkwater–A Family of Drinkwater of Cheshire, Lancashire, and the Isle of Man . . . , ed. by C. H. Drinkwater and W. G. D. Fletcher, printed by E. Dwelly, Fleet, 1920 (50).*

Druce—A Genealogical Account of the Family of Druce of Goreing . . . , by George Druce, 4to, London, 1735; 2nd edn., ed. by Charles Bridger, 4to, London, 1853 (50).

Drummond—Genealogy of the House of Drummond, by a Friend to Virtue and the Family (William Drummond), 1681.

Genealogy of the Most Noble and Ancient House of Drummond, by William 1st Viscount of Strathallan, 1681, with an appendix containing the Historie of the Familie of Perth, by Drummond of Hawthornden, ed. by David Laing, 4to, Edin., 1831 (100); also 4to, Glasgow, 1889 (100).

A Genealogical Memoir of the Most Noble and Ancient House of Drummond . . . , by David Malcolm, 12mo, Edin., 1808.

The Drummonds of Charing Cross, by Hector Bolitho and J. Peel, 1967.

Drury—History of the Family of Drury . . . Suffolk and Norfolk, by A. Campling, Mitchell Hughes and Clarke, 4to, 1937.

Du Cane—Some Account of the Family of Du Quesne, by Lt. Col. E. F. du Cane, 4to, London, 1876.

Duckett—Duchetiana . . . , by Sir G. F. Duckett Bt., 4to, London, 1869, enlarged edn., 4to, London, 1874-5.

The Duckett Family History, by T. E. Duckett, Bristol, 1961.

Dudley—The Sutton Dudleys of England . . . , by George Adlard, London, 1862.

Duff—Genealogical Memoirs of the Duffs . . . , by Sir William Baird of Auchmeddan (c. 1773), ed. by L. D. Gordon-Duff, Aberdeen, 1869.

The Book of the Duffs, by Alastair and Henrietta Tayler, 2v., 4to, Edin., 1914.

Dugdale—The Life . . . of Sir William Dugdale . . . , ed. by William Harper, London, 1827 (much genealogy).

Du Maurier—The Du Mauriers, by Daphne du Maurier, Gollancz, 1937.

Dundas—The Arniston Memoirs . . . , ed. by G. W. T. Omond, Edin., 1887.
Dundas of Fingask . . . , by Mrs Margaret I. Dundas, senior of Carronhall, Edin., 1891 (100).

Dunlop—Dunlop of that Ilk, Memorabilia . . . , by Archibald Dunlop, Glasgow, 1898.
Records of the Dunlops of Dunlop, by Robert Reid, Dunmow, 1900; 2nd edn. 1912.

Dunn—The Genealogies of the Dwnns of South Wales, by T. W. N. Dunn, Devizes, 1954.*

Durham—History of Altrincham and Bowdon . . . , with an Account of the House of Durham, by A. Ingram, Altrincham, 1879.

Durtnell—1496-1946: A Study in Continuity, by Lt. Col. C. S. Durtnell, O. B. E., Blades East and Blades, 1946.

Dutton—Historical and Genealogical Memoirs of the Dutton Family of Sherborne, by G. B. Morgan, introduction by Lord Sherborne, 4to, 1899 (25).*
Memorials of the Duttons of Dutton . . . , by G. B. Morgan, 4to, London and Chester, 4to, 1901.

Dwelly—Compendium of Notes on the Dwelly Family, by E. Dwelly, Fleet, 1912.

Dymock—Scrivelsby the Home of the Champions, with some

Account of the Marmyon and Dymoke Families, by the
Rev. S. Lodge, 4to, Horncastle, 1893; also 4to, London,
1894, and London, 1924.
See also Marmyun.

E

Eager—A Genealogical History of the Eager Family . . . , by F. J.
Eager, Dublin, 1861.

Eccles—The Eccles family, by J. Jeffreys, 1951.

Echlin—Memoirs of the Ancient Families of Echlin of Pittadro, by
George Crawfurd, Glasgow, 1747 (an appendix, n.d., brings
the pedigree down to 1820); revised and enlarged as a second
edition by the Rev. John R. Echlin, entitled Genealogical
Memoirs of the Echlin Family . . . , 72pp., Edin., 1882.*

Echyngham—Notices of the Family of Echyngham of Echyngham,
by Spencer T. Hall, London, 1850.

Ecroyd—See Vipont.

Eden—Some Historical Notes on the Eden Family . . . , by the
Rev. R. A. Eden, London, 1907.

Edgar—Genealogical Collections concerning the Scottish House
of Edgar, ed. by Andrew Edgar and C. Rogers, Grampian
Club, London, 1873.
Account of the Sirname of Edgar . . . Family of Wedderlie, by
Capt. J. H. Lawrence Archer, 4to, London, 1868.

Edgcumbe—Edgcumbe Family Records, by the Rev. J. Traherne,
Plymouth, 1888.

Edgeworth—The Black Book of Edgeworthstown and other Edge-

worth Memories, ed. by H. J. Butler and H. Edgworth
Butler, London, 1927.

Edmondstone—The Genealogy of the Lairds of Ednem and Duntreath from 1063 to 1699, 18mo, 15pp., Glasgow, 1699,
reprinted Berwick, 1790, and ed. by James Maidment,
Edin., 1834.
Genealogical Account of the Family of Edmondstone of
Duntreath, by Sir Archibald Edmondstone of Duntreath,
4to, Edin., 1875.*

Egerton—Descent and Alliances of William Egerton and his Heirs,
by Sir S. Egerton Brydges, fo., London, 1805.*
A Short Account of the Possessors of Oulton (Egerton and
Done Families), by Sir P. de Malpas Grey-Egerton, 4to,
1869 (20 copies on large paper).
The Bridgewater Millions, A Candid Family History, by B.
Falk, Hutchinson, 1942.

Elers—Memoirs of the Elers Family . . . , by Lt. Gen. E. H. D. E.
Napier, London, Taylor & Co., 1870.
Memoir of George Elers . . . with Genealogy and Notes, from
the original MS., by Lord Monson and G. Leveson-Gower,
London, Heinemann, 1903.

Eliot—The Border Eliots and the Family of Minto, by the hon.
G. F. S. Eliot, 4to, Edin., 1892 (125).*
Genealogical Memoranda relating to the Family of Eliot of
Port Eliot and Craggs of Wyserley, by Albert W. Woods, 4to,
1868.*
The Eliot Papers, compiled for the Family . . . , by Eliot Howard,
2v., 4to, Gloucester, 1893-5.
The Eliots of Burgh Wallis . . . , by Col. William Elliot, 4to, 1925.*
The Elliots . . . a Border Clan, by Lady Elliot, Seeley Service,
1974.

Elkington–The Elkingtons of Bath, by A. E. H. Elkington, Oxford,
     1965;* supplement, 1971.

Ellis–The Ellis Correspondence, by George Agar Ellis, London,
     1829 (vol. I. gives an account of the Family).
     Notices of the Ellises . . . , by W. Smith-Ellis, 2v., 4 supple-
     ments, London, 1857-81.*
     Notes of One Branch of the Ellis Family in Yorkshire and
     Leicestershire . . . , by E. Powell, 4to, London, 1905.*

Elmhirst–The Peculiar Inheritance, a History of the Elmhirsts,
     by Edward Elmhirst, Worsbrough, 1951.

Elphinstone–The Elphinstone Family Book . . . , by Sir William
     Fraser, 2v., 4to, Edin., 1897.*

Elsey–Genealogical Notes on the Elseys of Low Toynton . . . ,
     by W. M. Myddleton, 4to, Horncastle, 1915.*

Elton–See Mayo.

Elwell–The Iron Elwells, by C. J. L. Elwell, Ilfracombe, 1964.

Elwes–The Life of John Elwes Esq., with a Pedigree of the Family,
     by Edward Topham, London, 1790.
     An Account or History of all the Different Branches of the
     Elwes Family now Extant in England, by Dudley George
     Cary Elwes, 1866 (25).
     Genealogical Notices relating to the Elwes Family, London,
     1867.*
     Elsham and its Squires, by Daniel Rice, Derby, 1972.

Emerson–The English Emersons . . . , by P. H. Emerson, 4to,
     London, 1898 (250); also an edn. de luxe (50).*

Endecott–Devonshire Ancestry . . . of John Endecott, Governor of Massachusetts Bay in 1629, by Sir Roper Lethbridge (d. 1919).

Entwhistle–The Entwhistle Family, by B. Grimshaw, Accrington Gazette Co., 1924.*

Eoghan–A History of the Clan Eoghan, by R. F. Connelly, Dublin, 1864.*

Erskine–The Erskine-Halcro Genealogy . . . , by Ebenezer Erskine Scott, London, 1890; 2nd edn., Edin., 1895 (250).
The Erskines, by A. R. MacEwen, Edin., 1900.
The Lairds of Dun, by Violet Jacob, Murray, 1931.

Eskelby–The Genealogy of the Family of De Eskelby or Exelby, by Henry Douglas Eskelby, 4to, Birkenhead, 1891 (40).*

Evans–Genealogy of the Family of Evans of Montgomery, by J. R. Appleton and Morris C. Jones, Newcastle, 1865 (250).*
Annals of an Eton House, with some Notes on the Evans Family, by Maj. M. D. Gambier-Parry, Murray, 1907-8.

Evelyn–The History of the Evelyn Family, with a Special Memoir of William John Evelyn, M.P., by Helen Evelyn, London, 1915.

Ewen–The Families of Ewen of East Anglia and the Fenlands, by C. H. L'E. Ewen, 4to, 1928 (100).

Eyre–Memorials of the Eyre Family, by E. Phipps Eyre, Liverpool, 1885.*
A History of the Wiltshire Family of Eyre, by Mary E. F. Richardson-Eyre, 4to, London, 1897.
A History of the Family of Eyre of Eyrecourt, and Eyre of Eyreville in the co. of Galway, by the Rev. A. S. Hartigan, 2pts, Reading and London, 1898 and 1904.

Eyston—Pedigree of the Family of Eyston of East Hendred, by
C. I. Eyston, 4to, London, 1875.*

F

Fairbanks—The Fairbanks of Sheffield, by T. Walter Hall, Sheffield, 1932.

Falconer—Notes on the Family of Falconer, by Thomas Falconer,
Aberdare, 8pp., 1865-70 (often bound with Dalmahoy, q.v.).

Falkiner—A Pedigree, with Personal Sketches of the Falkiners of
Mount Falcon, comp. by F. B. Falkiner, Dublin, 1894.

Fanshawe—Genealogical and Historical Notes of the Fanshawe
Family, by Miss C. M. Fanshawe, 4to, 5pts, London, 1865-
72.*
The History of the Fanshawe Family, by H. C. Fanshawe and
Mrs Ridout, Newcastle, 1927.*

Faraday—The Faraday Genealogy, by J. E. and M. A. Faraday,
1967.

Farnham—Quorndon Records, collected by George F. Farnham,
4to, 1912.

Farquharson—Records of Invercauld 1541-1828, ed. by the Rev.
J. G. Michie, New Spalding Club, 1901.
Farquharson Genealogies, by A. M. Mackintosh, Nairn, Pt. 1, Ach-
riachen Branch, 1913; Pt. 2, Inverey Branch, 1914 (100 each).

Farrer—Some Farrer Memorials 1610-1923, by Thomas, 2nd Lord
Farrer, London, 1923.*

Fasken—The Family of Fasken, by Brig. Gen. W. H. Fasken, C.B.,
Stroud News, 1931.*

Fawcett—Fawcett of no fixed abode, by A. W. P. Fawcett, Barnet, 1966.

Fawkes—The Fawkes of York . . . , by Robert Davies, 12mo, Westminster, 1850.

Feather—Collections relating to the Surname of Feather, by G. W. Marshall, paper covers, Worksop, 1887, facsimile reprint 1972 (150).

Fell—The Fells of Swarthmore Hall . . . , by Maria Webb, London, 1865, 2nd edn., 1867 (also Philadelphia, 1884).

Fellowes—The Family and Descent of William Fellowes of Eggesford, by the Rev. E. H. Fellowes, 4to, 1910.

Fenwick—The Fate of the Fenwicks, ed. by A. F. Wedd, London, 1927.
The Fenwicks of Northumberland, by B. Fenwick, 1930.

Fergusson—Records of the Clan and Name of Fergusson . . . , ed. for the Clan Fergusson Society by James Fergusson and the Rev. R. M. Fergusson, 1895; Supplement, Edin., D. Douglas, 1899.
The Fergussons, their Lowland and Highland Branches, by Sir James Fergusson, Edin., 1956.

Ferrers—Baddesley Clinton . . . , with some Account of the family of Ferrers . . . , by the Rev. Henry Norris, 4to, London, and Leamington, 1897.
The Ferrers Family History . . . , by C. S. F. Ferrers, 4to, 1899.*

Few—The Fews of Cambridgeshire: A Family History, by Arthur J. Gautrey, Eastbourne, 1972.

ffarington—ffaringtons of Farington and Worden, by S. M. ffarington, 1936.

ffooks–The Family of ffooks of Sherborne, by E. C. ffooks, 1958.*

fforde–Parentalia: Reminiscences of . . . fforde of fforde Green etc., by Frederick Forde, 4to, London, 1878 (40).*

Field–The Field Family of Tamworth, by Thomas Kemp, Birmingham, 1910.

Fielden–A Genealogical Memorial of the Family of Fielden . . . , by Henry Fishwick, 4to, London, 1884 (12).

Filmer–Seven Centuries of a Kent Family, by John L. Filmer, 1975.

Finch–The History of Burley-on-the-Hill, Rutland, by Pearl Finch, London, 1901 (chiefly a history of the Finch Family).
   The History of the Finch Family, by Bryan l'Anson, 4to, 1933 (250).

Fisher–De Stemmata Piscatoris . . . , by Frank Owen Fisher, 4to, 1910 (re the Fishers of Tidd).

Fiske–The Fiske Family Papers, by Henry ffiske, 4to, Norwich, 1902.*

Fitzgerald–Initium, Incrementa, et Exitus Familiae Geraldinorum Desmoniae Comitium, etc., par Frat. Dominic de Rosario O'Daly, Ulyssipone, Ex Officina Craesbeecksiana. 12mo, 1655; French edn., Dunkerque, 1697, a translation by C. P. Meeham, 12mo, Dublin, 1847.
   The Earls of Kildare and their Ancestors, 1057-1773, by the Marquess of Kildare, Dublin, 1857; 2nd edn., Dublin, 1858;

3rd edn., with additions, 1862; 4th edn., 1864; the final part, Descent of the Earls of Kildare, re-issued 1869.
The Geraldines, by Brian Fitzgerald, 1951.

Fitzherbert—The Fitzherberts of Somersal, by S. T. Fitzherbert, Chiswick Press, 1922.

Fitzmaurice—See Petty-Fitzmaurice.

Fitzroy—The Royal Fitzroys, Dukes of Grafton . . . , by Bernard Falk, 1950.

FitzWalter—The History of the Noble Robert FitzWalter, Lord of Woodham in Essex, and of his Ancestors, by W. V., 4to, London, 1616.

Fleetwood—Fleetwood Family Records, collected and edited by R. W. Buss, complete in 7pts, 4to, wrappers, 1914-21.
The Ancestry of William Fleetwood, Bishop of St Asaph and Ely . . . , by R. W. Buss, London, 1926.
The Family of Fleetwood of Calwich, co. Stafford . . . , by R. W. Buss, London, 1908 (100).*

Fleming—Historical . . . Memoirs of the Family of Fleming of Slane, by Sir W. Betham, fo., Dublin, 1829.*
Biggar and the House of Fleming, by William Hunter, Biggar, 4to, 1862; 2nd edn., Edin., 1867.

Fletcher—The Collections of the Family of Fletcher of Saltoun, 4to, 8pp., Edin., 1803, reprinted 4to, Haddington, 1896.
See also Longridge.

Flint—Brief Records of the Flint Family, by B. F. Flint, 1856.*

Fold—The Folds of Danehouse, by W. Folds Hall, 1960 (100).

Foljambe—Notices of the Family of Foljambe, by N. Johnson, 1701.

Folkard—A Monograph of the Family of Folkard of Suffolk, by Arthur C. Folkard, 4to, 3ots, 1890-7 (40).*

Folliott—The Folliotts of Londonderry and Chester, by Sir E. T. Bewley, ? Dublin, c. 1900.
History of the ffolliott Family, by R. Staveley, fo., Oxford, 1914.*

Forbes—Genealogy of the Family of Forbes, by Mathew Lumsden of Tullicarn, 1580, ed. by William Forbes, large paper 4to, Inverness, 1819, reprinted 1883.
The Genealogy of the House of Tolquhon, by J. Davidson, 21pp., Aberdeen, Constitutional Office, 1839.
Memoranda Relating to the Family of Forbes of Waterton, by John Forbes (b. 1754), 4to, 61pp., Aberdeen, 1857.*
Memoirs of a Banking House, by Sir William Forbes of Pitsligo, 1860.
Memorials of the Family of Forbes of Forbesfield . . . , by Alexander Forbes, small 4to, Aberdeen, 1905 (150).*
The House of Forbes, ed. by Alastair and Henrietta Tayler, Third Spalding Club, 1937.

Forbes-Robertson—The Picturesque Ancestry of Sir Johnston Forbes Robertson, by J. M. Bulloch, Aberdeen, 1926.

Ford—See fforde.

Fordyce—See Dingwall.

Forrest—A History of the Forrest Family of Birmingham and Shrewsbury, by H. E. Forrest, 4to, Wellington, Salop, 1923 (130).

Forster, Foster—Epistolarium, or Fasciculi of Curious Letters

..., and some Account ... of the Forster Family, by T.
Ignatius Forster, 3v. in 1, Bruges, 1845-52.

Some Account of the Pedigree of the Forsters of Cold Hesle-
don, co. Durham, by Joseph Foster, Sunderland, 4to,
1862.*

Genealogy of the Descendants of Roger Foster of Edreston, Northumberland, by A. H. Foster-Barham, London, 4to, 1897.

Notes on the Foster Family of Dowsby and Moulton, co. Lincs.,
comp. by Green, 1875; 2nd edn., by W. E. Foster, 4to, 1907
(an appendix, 4to, Guildford, 1909*).

Forsyth—A Family Memoir, by Dorothea Forsyth, 1939.

Fortescue—The History of the Family of Fortescue in all its
Branches, by Thomas Fortescue, Lord Clermont, 2v. and
Supp., fo., London, 1869, 2nd edn. thick 4to, Edin.,
1880.

Fothergill—The Fothergills of Ravenstonedale, by Catherine Thornton and Frances McLaughlin, London, 1905.

Fowler—A Short Account of the Fowler Family, by Jean E. Fowler, 4to, 1897.*

Fox—A Short Genealogical Account of Some of the Various Families of Fox in the West of England ..., by C. H. Fox, 4to,
Bristol, 1864.*

A Revised Genealogical Account of the Various Families descended from Francis Fox of St Germans, by Joseph Foster,
4to, London, 1872.

Genealogical Memoranda relating to the Family of Fox, of Bris-
lington, 4to, London, 1871-2; 2nd edn., 2pts., 4to, Bristol
and Edin., 1884-97.

Fraser—The True Genealogy of the Frasers 916-1674, by the Rev.
James Fraser, (Wardlaw MS), ed. by William Mackay for the

Scottish Hist. Soc., 1905.

Annals . . . Distinguished Family of Fraser . . . , by Archibald Simson, Edin., 1795; 2nd edn., ed. by Col. A. Frazer, 1805.*

Historical Account of the Family of Frisel or Fraser . . . , by John Anderson, 4to, Edin., 1825.

The Frasers of Philorth, by Alexander Fraser, 17th Lord Saltoun, 4to, 3v., Edin., 1879 (150).*

Historical Account of the Frasers of Lovat . . . , by Alexander Mackenzie, 4to, Inverness, 1896.

The Land and Lairds of Touch, by J. C. Gibson, Stirling, 1929.

Frederick—The Family of Frederick, by Edmund H. Fellowes, 1932 (100).*

Freke—A Pedigree or Genealogy of the Family of the Frekes . . . , by Ralph Freke of Hannington, 'secondly augmented' by the Rev. John Freke . . . and William Freke . . . 1707, printed by Sir Thomas Phillipps, fo., 1825.

French—Memoir of the Family of French . . . , by John D'Alton, Dublin, 1847; additions by Phillip More, 4pp, 1855.

The Family of French of Belturbet and Nixon of Fermanagh, by the Rev. H. B. Swanzy, Dublin, 1908.*

Frere—Parentalia, being a Pedigree of the Family of Frere of Norfolk and Suffolk, 4to, 1843; another edition by J. G. Frere, 1965.

Pedigree of the Family of Frere of Roydon . . . , by Horace Frere, 4to, 1874*; 2nd edn. comp. by H. and A. H. Frere, 4to, Eyre & Spottiswoode, 1899.

Fuller—The Family of Fuller, some . . . Descents of the Kerry Branch, by James Franklin Fuller, fo., Dublin, 1880 (20).

Fulton—Memoirs of the Fultons of Lisburn, comp. by Sir T. C.

Hope, 4to, 1903.*

Fynes-Clinton—Annals of our Ancestors . . . , by A. R. Craik, 1924 (100).
See also Clinton.

Fynmore—Memorials of the Family of Fynmore with Notes on the Origin . . . , by W. P. W. Phillimore, London, 1886.
See also Phillimore.

G

Gainsford—Annals of the House of Gainsford . . . , ed. by W. D. Gainsford, fo., Horncastle, 1904-9 (50).*

Gairdner—A Chronicle of the Family of Gairdner, by W. H. Bailey, 1947.

Gale—Reliquae Galeaniae . . . , by Roger and Samuel Gale, 4to, 1781.

Galpin—The Family of Galpin of Staffordshire and Dorset . . . , by G. L. Galpin, Chiswick Press, 1926.*

Galwey—The Galweys of Lota, by C. J. B. Bennett, Dublin, 1909.

Garnier—The Chronicles of the Garniers of Hampshire . . . , by A. E. Garnier, 4to, Norwich and London, 1900.

Garstang—From Generation to Generation . . . Garstangs of Lancashire, by S. G. Gurney, London, 1970.

Gautrey—The Gautreys of Cambridgeshire . . . , by A. J. Gautrey, 1969.*

Gayer—Memoirs of the Family of Gayer, comp. by A. B. Gayer,

4to, Westminster, 1870.*

Gayre—Gayre's Book, by G. R. Gayre, and R. L. Gair, 3v., Philli-more, 1948-54; vol. 4, Oliver and Boyd, 1959.

Geddes—The Forging of a Family, by A. C. Geddes, Faber, 1952.

Gee—Gee of Freshford and London, by H. Gee, 4to, Chiswick Press, 1916.

Gemmil—Notes on the Probable Origin of the Scottish Surname of Gemmil or Gemmell, with a Genealogical Account of the Family of Gemmil of Templehouse, by J. Gemmil, Montreal and Ottawa, 4to, 1898-1901.
(the same) . . . with a Genealogical Account of the Family of Gemmil of Raithmuir, Fenwick, by J. Leiper Gemmil, 4to, Glasgow, 1909.*

George—See Gorges.

Gibb—The Life and Times of Robert Gibb, Lord of Carriber . . . , with a Notice of his Descendants . . . , by Sir G. D. Gibb, Bt., of Falkland, 2v., 1874.

Gibbins—Record of the Gibbins Family . . . , by Emma Gibbins, 4to, Birmingham, 1911.*

Gibbons—Gibbons Family Notes . . . , by A. W. Gibbons, West-minster, 1884 (30).*

Gibbs—Pedigree of the Family of Gibbs of Clyst St George . . . , by Henry H. Gibbs, fo., wrapper, London, 1890; 2nd edn., ed. by Lord Aldenham, 1904*; 3rd edn., by Vicary A. Gibbs, Michell Hughes & Clarke, 1932.
The History of Gibbs of Felton in Dartington, co. Devon, by Lord Hunsdon of Hunsdon, London, St Catherine Press,

1925-6 (150).
The History of Antony and Dorothea Gibbs . . . , by J. A. Gibbs, 4to, London, 1922 (100).

Gibson–Some Notes on the Family of Gibson of Glencrosh, by T. M. Fallow, Dumfries, 1905.*

Giffard–The Tombs of the Giffards, with a Pedigree of the Family, by J. Hicks Smith, Wolverhampton, 1870.

Gilbert–The Family and Arms of Gilbert of Colchester, by S. P. Thompson, 4to, wrapper, 1904.

Giles–Aegidiana, or Gleanings among the Gileses . . . , by One of Them (A. H. Giles), London, 1910.*

Gill–The Genealogy of the Family of Gylle or Gill of Hertfordshire, Essex, and Kent . . . , by Gordon Gyll, 4to, London, 1842.
Account of the Family of Gill of Blairythan and Savock, by A. J. Michell Gill, ? Edin., 1882-4.

Gilman–Records of the Gilman Family, by A. Gilman, 1863.*
The Gillmans of Highgate, with Letters from S. T. Coleridge . . . , by A. W. Gillman, 4to, London, 1895.
Searches into the History of the Gillman or Gilman Family, by A. W. Gillman, 2v., 4to, 1895-6.

Gilpin–Memoirs of Dr Richard Gilpin of Scaleby Castle in Cumberland . . . and of his Posterity . . . , by the Rev. W. Gilpin, 1791; 2nd edn., ed. by William Jackson, London, 1879.

Girdlestone–Genealogical Notes on the Girdlestone Family, by R. R. Girdlestone, Eyre and Spottiswoode, 1904.

Glanville–Records of the Anglo-Norman House of Glanville,

1050-1880, by W. V. S. Glanville Richards, 4to, London, 1882.

Glazebrook—The Earliest Glazebrooks and their Norman Origin, by C. J. Glazebrook, 1969; 2nd edn. 1971 as The Mediaeval Origin of the Glazebrooks.

Gledstone—The Gledstones and the Siege of Cocklaw, by Mrs Oliver of Thornwood, Edin., 1878.

Glen—Memorials of the Scottish Family of Glen, by the Rev. Charles Rogers, Edin., 1888.*

Glendinning—The House of Glendinning, 4to, 1879.*

Glendour—The History of the Island of Anglesey with the Memoirs and Genealogical Account of Owen Glendour, 4to, 1775.

Glover—The Pedigree and Arms of the Glovers of Mount Glover, by D. O. C. Fisher and Sir J. B. Burke, London, 1858.

Glynne—The Glynnes of Hawarden, by W. E. B. Whittaker, 1906.

Goddard—Memoirs of the Goddards of North Wiltshire . . . , by Richard Jefferies, 4to, Swindon and London, 1873.*

Godman—Some Account of the Family of Godman . . . , by Percy S. Godman, 4to, London, 1897.*
Appendix to the above, Mitchell Hughes and Clarke, 1916.

Godolphin—The Godolphins, by Brig. Gen. F. G. Marsh, C.M.G., D.S.O., Salisbury, W. H. Smith, 1930.*

Goldesborough—Memorials of the Goldesborough Family, by Albert Goldesborough, Aldenham and London, 1930.*

Goldney—A House and a Family, by P. K. Stembridge, Bristol, 1969.*

Goodall—See Young.

Goodchild—The Family of Goodchild of Pallion Hall . . . , by H. R. Leighton, Sunderland, 1904.

Goodricke—History of the Goodricke Family, ed. by C. A. Goodricke, 4to, 2v., London, 1885-91.*

Goodwyn—The Goodwyns of Lynn Regis, Norfolk, by H. W. Goodwyn of Milford Lodge, Lymington, 4to, 1876.

Gordon—The History of the Ancient, Noble, and Illustrious Family of Gordon . . . , by William Gordon of Old Aberdeen, 2v., Edin., 1726-7.

Concise History of the Ancient and Illustrious House of Gordon, by C. A. Gordon, 12mo., Aberdeen, 1754; reprinted Aberdeen, 1890.

A Genealogical History of the Earldom of Sutherland . . . to the year 1630, by Sir Robert Gordon, Bt. of Gordonstoun (with a continuation to 1651), published from the original MS and edited by Henry Weber, fo., Edin., 1813.

The Sutherland Book, by Sir William Fraser, 4to, 3v., 1892.

Memorials of the Family of Gordon of Lesmoir, by D. Wimberley, Inverness, 1893.*

Gordon Memoirs, 1745-1887, by S. E. R. Gordon, 12mo., 1895.*

Notes on the Family of Gordon of Terpersie . . . , by D. Wimberley, Inverness, 1900.

The Crougly Book, by G. H. H. B. Gordon, London, 1895.

Llwyn-y-Bwch . . . Gordon of Gower . . . , comp. by the Rev. J. D. Davies, Swansea, 1903.

The House of Gordon, ed. by J. M. Bulloch, 4to, 3v., New Spalding Club, 1903-07-12.

A Genealogical Account of the Family of Knockespock, by
   D. Wimberley, Banff, 1903.*
Memorials of the Family of Gordon of Craig, by D. Wimberley,
   Banff, 1904.
A Short History of the Later Gordons of Baldorney, by D.
   Wimberley, Banff, 1904.
The Gordons of Craiglaw (Memorial Volume), by William Mac-
   Math, ed. by T. Fraser, 4to, Dalbeattie, 1924 (175).
The Gordons of Birkenburn, by James George, Keith, 1912.
Note: For other works, especially by T. M. Bulloch and D. Wimber-
   ley, see Margaret Stuart, Scottish Family History, 1930.

Gordon-Clark—The Family of Gordon-Clark, by C. P. Gordon-
   Clark, Saffron Walden, 1972.

Gorges—Pedigrees and History of the Family of George and
   Gorges, by Major T. George, 4to, 1903.*

Gorham—Genealogical Account of the Breton and Anglo-Breton
   Families of de Gorram . . . , by the Rev. George C. Gorham,
   London, 1837.

Gorton—The Gortons of Gorton . . . , by J. Higson, London, 1873.*

Gough—The Goughs of Hyddle, co. Salop, by F. H. Gough, 1893.

Goulden—The Gouldens of Canterbury 1686-1947, by A. T. Goulden, Tunbridge Wells, 19—.

Gourlay—Memorials of the Scottish House of Gourlay, by the
   Rev. Charles Rogers, 4to, Edin., 1888.
The Gourlays of Dundee, by S. G. E. Lythe, 1965.

Gournay—Three Hundred Years of a Norman House; the Barons
   of Gournay . . . , by James Hannay, London, 1867.
The Record of the House of Gournay . . . , by Daniel Gurney,

4to, 4pts in 3v., 1848. Supplement entitled The Gurneys of
St Benet Fink, London, and Maldon Essex, by C. A. Bernau,
4to, 1858.

The House of Gournay . . . , by T. J. Pettigrew, 4to, 186—.

See also Gurney and Yvery.

Grace—A Survey of Tullaroan . . . , being a Genealogical History
of the Family of Grace, Dublin, 1819 (50).

Memoirs of the Family of Grace, by Sheffield Grace, 2v.,
London, 1823;* 6 copies on tinted paper, and 25 copies
thick 4to.

The Family of Grace, Pedigrees and Memoirs, collected and
edited by the Rev. J. Willhelm, fo., 1911.*

Graham—The Red Book of Monteith, by W. Fraser, 4to, 2v.,
Edin., 1880.

The Red Book . . . Reviewed . . . , by George Burnett, 4to,
Edin., 1881.

The Grahams of Gartmore, by Alexander C. McIntyre, 4to,
Glasgow, 1885.*

The Grahams of Wallacetown, by James Graham, Glasgow,
1887.

The Grahams of Tamrawer, by J. E. Graham, Edin., 1895 and
1903.*

Or and Sable: a Book of the Graemes and Grahams, by
Louisa G. Graeme, 4to, Edin., 1903 (295), ? another edition, 1919.

Graham of Claverhouse, by Michael Barrington, London, 1911.

The Grahams of Auchencloich and Tamrawer, by J. St J. N.
Graham, Lisbon, 1952.

The Grahams of Kirkstall, by Canon W. H. Mackean, 1960.*

Grant—Memoires Historiques . . . de la Maison de Grant of Scotland . . . , by Charles, Vicomte de Vaux, London, 1796.

Genealogy of the Honourable Family of Grant of Grant, by J.
Grant, 4to, Elgin, 23pp., 1826.

An Account of the Rise and Offspring of the Name of Grant,
by Sir A. Grant, 1876.*

The Chiefs of Grant, by Sir W. Fraser, 4to, 3v., Edin., 1883.

Reminiscences . . . of the Grants of Glenmoriston, by the Rev.
A. Sinclair, 4to, Edin., 1887.

The Grants of Corrimony, by Francis J. Grant, Lerwick, 4to,
1895.

The Rulers of Strathspey . . . , by the Earl of Cassillis, Inverness, 1911; also a 4to edn. de luxe.

The Clan Grant, by I. F. Grant, Edin., 1955.

Grantham—The Genealogie of the Severall Branches of the
Auntient Name and Family of Grantham of Goltho . . .
1652, London, 1852 (25).*

Granville—History of the Granville Family traced back to Rollo
. . . , by the Rev. R. G. Granville, 4to, Exeter, 1895.

See also Round, Family Origins, 1970, p. 130 et seq.

Graves—Graves Memoirs of the Civil War . . . , by F. A. Bates, 4to,
London, 1927.

Gray—Skibo, its Lairds and History, by Peter Gray, Edin., 1906.

Papers and Diaries of a York Family 1764-1839, by Mrs
Edwin Gray, London, 1927.

See also Grey.

Green—A Memoir of Thomas Green Esq. of Ipswich and an
Account of his Family and Connections, by James Ford,
4to, Ipswich, 1825 (100).

Succinct Genealogical Proofs of the House of Greene that
were Lords of Drayton . . . 1685, by R. Halstead (Earl of
Peterborough), photographic facsimile, etc., with Introduction by F. V. Greene, fo., London, 1896.

The Family of Green of Youghal, co. Cork . . . , by the Rev.
H. B. Swanzy and T. G. H. Green, Dublin, 1902.*

Francis Green of Denmark Hill and his Descendants, by
C. A. H. Green, Bishop of Monmouth, 1926; 2nd edn.,
1928.

Greenhalgh—Memoranda of the Greenhalgh Family, by J. D.
Greenhalgh, Bolton, 1869 and 1877;* facsimile reprint,
London, 1971.

Greenstreet—Memorials of the Ancient Kent Family of Greenstreet, collected by James Greenstreet, 1891.

Gregory—A Short Account of the Family of Gregorie . . . , by
Henry Gregory (printed by Miss Georgina Gregory 'for my
great nephew Henry Gregory'), 1873 (25).*
Records of the Family of Gregory, by Sir P. S. Gregory, 4to,
London, 1886.*
The House of Gregory, by V. R. T. Gregory, Dublin, 1943.

Grelley—Observations on the Armorial Beaings of the Town of
Manchester, and of the Descent of the . . . Family of Grelley,
by W. R. Whatton, 4to, Manchester, 1824.*

Gresham—Genealogical Memoranda relating to the Family of
Gresham, comp. by G. Leveson-Gower, 4to, London, pts.
1-3, 1874-6; 2nd issue, fo., 1883.*

Gresley—The Gresleys of Drakelowe . . . , by Falconer Madan,
Oxford, 1899* (printed as pt. 1 of the Hist. Collns. Staffs.
N.S. 1) (Wm. Salt Arch. Soc.); also a special edn., 4to,
1899.

Greville—Historical and Genealogical Account of the Noble
Family of Greville . . . , ed. by J. Edmondson, London,
1766.*

Grey—The Milfield MS, or a Genealogical and Historical Account

of the Grey Family of Northumberland, with Notes . . . ,
   by E. Hepple, 4to, 1856.*
Bradgate House, the Greys of Groby . . . , by J. D. Paul, Leicester, 1899.
See also Gray.

Griffin—The Griffins of Dingley . . . , by J. Harvey Bloom, 1921.

Griffith—The Family of Griffith of Garn and Plasnewydd . . . ,
   ed. by T. A. Glenn, Harrison & Sons, 1935 (95).

Grimston—Leaves from a Family Tree, by M. E. Ingram,
   1951.

Groundwater—Memories of an Orkney Family, by Henrietta
   Groundwater, Kirkwall, 1867.

Grove—The Grove Family of Halesowen, by the Rev. James Davenport, London, 1912.

Grubbe—Genealogical Memoranda of the Grubbe Family, 4to,
   1893.*

Gubbins—Memoirs of the Gubbins Family, by G. G. Gubbins,
   Limerick, 1891.

Guiness—The Guiness Family, by H. S. and B. Guiness, 2v., 1953.

Guise—Autobiography of Thomas Raymond, and Memoirs of the
   Family of Guise of Elmore, Glos., ed. by G. G. Davies, 4to,
   Camden Soc., 1917.

Gundry—Notes on the Gundry Family, comp. by W. G. C. Gundry,
   4to, Gay and Hancock, 1922 (a very few copies).

Gunn—The Gunns, by T. Sinclair, 4to, Wick, 1890.

History of the Clan Gunn, by Mark Rugg Gunn, Glasgow, 1969.

Gunning—Documents of the Gunning Family . . . , by George
     Gunning, Cheltenham, 1834.*
Genealogy of the Gunning Family, by C. J. H. Gunning and
     A. Warder, fo., 1907.

Gurney—The Gurneys of Earlham, by A. J. C. Hare, 2v., London,
     1895; 2nd edn., 1897.
Some Particulars of the Lives of William Brodie Gurney and
     his Immediate Ancestors, written chiefly by Himself,
     Gresham Press, 1902.*
See also Gournay.

Guthrie—Genealogy of the Descendants of the Rev. Thomas
     Guthrie, D. D. . . . , by C. J. Guthrie, 4to, Edin., 1902.
The Guthrie Family, ed. by D. C. Guthrie and the Hon. Mrs
     Stuart Wortley, 4to, 1906.*

Gwatkin—The Gwatkins of Herefordshire, by E. M. Gwatkin and
     G. F. T. Sherwood, London, 1914 (50).

H

Hadden—A Short Narrative of the Life . . . of an Aberdonian, to
     which is added an Account of the Hadden Family, by J. D.
     Tough, Aberdeen, 1848.

Haddock—Correspondence of the Family of Haddock, 1657-1719,
     ed. by E. M. Thompson, Camden Soc., 1881.
The Descendants of John Haddock, by Sir D. Gamble, 1897.

Haddon—A History of the Haddons of Naseby . . . , by the Rev.
     W. G. Cruft and Walter Haddon, 4to, London, 1915.

Haig—The Haigs of Bemersyde . . . , by John Russell, Blackwood,

1881.

Tyde What May . . . , ed. by Mrs Alexander Stuart, 5pts, 4to, Edin., 1894, 1895, 1900.

Haime—The Haimes, a Dorset Family, by the Rev. John W. Haime, Wimborne, 1970 (500).

Haines—A Complete Memoir of Richard Haines . . . , with a Full Account of His Ancestry and Posterity, by C. R. Haines, London, 1899 (250).*

Haldane—Memoranda Relative to the Family of Haldane of Gleneagles, by Alexander Haldane, fo., London, 1880.
The Haldanes of Gleneagles, by Gen. Sir J. A. L. Haldane, 4to, Edin., Blackwood, 1929.

Hale—The Family of Hale of Bristol, by W. M. Hale, 4to, Bickers, 1936.*

Haliburton—Memorials of the Haliburtons, by Sir Walter Scott, Bt., 4to, Edin., 1820, 1824, 1842-3.

Halkerston—A Genealogical Account of the Family of Halkerston of that Ilk, ? by Helenus Halkerston, 15pp., 1772.

Hall—The Hall Family, by R. H. Warren, Bristol, 1910 (100).*
See also King-Hall.

Hallen—An Account of the Family of Hallen or Holland . . . , by the Rev. A. W. C. Hallen, 4to, Edin., 1885 (100).*

Halley—The Halley and Pyke Families, by E. F. M. Pike, 1910.

Hamilton—Historical and Genealogical Memoirs of the House of Hamilton . . . , by John Anderson, 4to, Edin., 1825; supplement, 4to, 1827.

'Memoirs of the House of Hamilton', corrected, with an addition, by Dr F. H. Hamilton of Bardowie, 4to, Edin., 1828.

Reply to the Misstatements of Doctor Hamilton of Bardowie . . . , by John Riddell, 4to, Edin., 1828.

An Inquiry into the Pedigree, Descent . . . of the Chiefs of the Hamilton Family, by Walter Aiton, Glasgow, 1827.

Hamilton Memoirs . . . , (Ireland), comp. by Everard Hamilton, 4to, 2v., 1889-91; 2nd edn., 4to, Dundalk, 1920.

A Short Account of the Hamiltons of Bargany, by the Hon. H. H. Dalrymple, 4to, 1897.*

The Hamiltons of Fala . . . , by the Hon. H. H. Dalrymple, 1907.*

A History of the House of Hamilton, by Lt. Col. George Hamilton, Edin., Skinner, 1933.

See also Birnie.

Hamley—The Family of Hamley, Hambly, and Hambling, by Edmund H. Hambly, Gloucester, 1945.*

Hamlyn—History of the Suburbs of Exeter . . . with a Special Notice of the Hamlyn Family, by Charles Worthy, Exeter, 1892.

Hanbury—The Hanbury Family, by A. A. Locke, 2v., fo., London, Humphrey, 1916-7.

Hanmer—Notes and Papers to serve for a Memorial of the Parish of Hanmer in Flintshire, collected by Sir John Hanmer, Bt., 1872 2nd edn., 4to, Westminster, 1876-7* (in large part devoted to the genealogy of the Hanmer Family).

The Hanmers of Morton and Montford . . . , by Calvert Hanmer, 4to, London, 1916.

Hannay—The Hannays of Sorbie, by Francis Stuart, London, 1961.

Harben—See Chamberlain.

Harcourt—Histoire Généalogique de la Maison de Harcourt, par
    M. De la Roque, Paris, 4v., fo., 1662.
  Harcuria, A History of the Family of Harcourt, by W. H. Bath,
    1930.

Harding—Some Account of the Family of Harding of Cranmore,
    by R. D. Reid, 1917.

Hardwick—History of the Family of Hardwick . . . , by Herbert
    Junius Hardwicke, Sheffield, 1878.*
  Hardwycke Annals (co. Derby), by Ambrose Trusswell Turner, 1905.*
  Hardwicke of Hardwicke and Burcott, by J. W. H-Jones, 1911.

Hardy—The Hardys of Barbon. . . , by C. F. Hardy, London, 1913.

Harford—Annals of the Harford Family, ed. by Alice Harford,
    n.d.; 2nd edn., 4to, London, 1909.*

Harley—Account of the Harley Family, by Arthur Collins, 4to, 1741.
  See also Cavendish.

Harrington—The Harrington Family, by Ian Grimble, Cape, 1957.
  See also Bave.

Harris—Family Memorials. . . , ed. by Mary Anne Harris, n.p., 1869.*
  A Narrative of the Descendants . . . Harris . . . of Fording-
    bridge . . . with a Notice of the Family of Masterman of
    London, by Joseph Foster, London, 1878* (also 4to, 1895
    with a slightly different title).

Harrison—The House of Harrison . . . , by C. R. and H. G. Harrison,
    issued by Harrisons, printers to the King, 4to, 1914.
  The Early History of the Harrisons of Freckleton, co. Lancs.,
    by Cdr. M. J. Harrison, R.N., 1922.*
  The Harrisons of Newton and Bankfield in Lancashire, by
    C. W. Harrison, Exeter, Pollard, 1939.*

See also Branfill.

Hart—The Family History of Hart of Donegal, by H. T. Hart,
  London, 1907 (60).
See also Shakespeare.

Harvey—Genealogy of the Family of Harvey of Folkstone, by
  W. J. Harvey, 4to, London, 1889 (50).*
The Harvey Families of Inishowen, co. Donegal and Maen, co.
  Cornwall, by Lt. Col. G. H. Harvey, 4to, Folkstone, 1927-8
  (100).

Harward—Hereward, the Saxon Patriot; . . . a Record of His
  Ancestors and Descendants 445-1896, by Lt. Gen. Harward,
  4to, London, 1896.
See also Round, Peerage and Family History, p. 80.

Haslewood—The Genealogy of the Family of Haslewood of Wick-
  warren . . . by the Rev. F. Haslewood, 4to, wrapper, London,
  1875.
Genealogy of the Family of Haslewood, Warwickshire and
  Staffordshire Branch . . . , by the Rev. F. Haslewood, 4to,
  London, 1881.*

Hassard—History and Genealogy of the Hassards, by the Rev. H.
  Hassard Short, 4to, York, 1858.
Some Account of the Family of Hassard . . . , by the Rev. H. B.
  Swanzy, Dublin, 1903.*

Hastings—The Huntingdon Peerage . . . a History of the House of
  Hastings, by H. N. Bell, 4to, London, 1820; 2nd edn., 1821.
Hastings of Hastings, by R. J. Beevor, 1931.
Hastings Saga (Hastings of Wenham), by M. A. H. Marshall,
  1953.

Haward—The Hawardes of Tandridge, co. Surrey, by W. Paley

Baildon, 1894.

Hawkins—The Hawkins Family (Plymouth Armada Heroes), by
Mary W. S. Hawkins, 4to, Plymouth, 1888, and 4to, London,
1890.
The Hawkins Dynasty, by Michael Lewis, G. Allen and Unwin,
1969.

Hawley—Genealogy of the Hawley Family of Marblehead, by W. D.
Hawley, 1887.*

Haws—The Haws Family and Their Seafaring Kin, by Capt. G. W.
Haws, 12mo., Dunfermline, Mackie and Co., 1932.*

Hawtrey—The History of the Hawtrey Family, by F. M. Hawtrey,
2v., London, 1903.

Hay—De Nobilissimae Gentis Hayorum origine, Carmen Histor-
icum, by James Ross, 12mo., Edin., 1700 and 1703.
Historical Account of the Family of Hay of Leys, by
Alexander Deuchar, fo., Edin., 1832.
Genealogie of the Hayes of Tweedale, by Father R. A. Hay,
ed. by James Maidment, 4to, Edin., 1835 (108, and 12 on
large paper).
The Family of Hay of Duns Castle, by F. S. Day, Edin., 1922.

Haydock—The Haydock Papers, by Joseph Gillow, 4to, London,
1888.

Hazlitt—Four Generations of a Literary Family, the Hazlitts in
England, Ireland, and America, 1725-1896, by W. Carew
Hazlitt, 2v., London and New York, 1897. (Withdrawn
by the publisher on the day of issue, and issued later in 1 v.,
as The Hazlitts, 1911.)

Head—The Families of Head and Somerville, by J. Cameron Head,

1917 (20).

Heal—Heal Family Records, by A. and E. Heal, 1932.*

Heape—Records of the Family of Heape of Heape, Staley, Saddle-
worth and Rochdale from 1170 to 1905, by C. and R.
Heape, 4to, 1905.*

Hearsey—The Hearseys: Five Generations of an Anglo-Indian
Family, by Col. Hugh Pearse, D.S.O., 1905.

Heath—Heathiana . . . , by Sir W. R. Drake, London, fo., 1881*;
revd edn., London, 1882 (privately printed for Baron
Heath from 'Devon Notes and Notelets').
Records of the Heath Family . . . , by G. Heath, 4to, 1913.*
The Pedigree of the Heath Family of Kepyer and Little Eden,
co. Durham etc., by C. R. Everett and C. Masterman, 4to,
1914.

Heathcote—An Account of Some of the Families bearing the
Name of Heathcote . . . co. Derby, by E. D. Heathcote, 4to,
1899 (200).

Henham—See King.

Hennicker—See Major.

Henry—The Descendants of Philip Henry, M.A., incumbent of
Worthenbury, co. Flint . . . , by Sarah Lawrence, London,
1844.

Henzy—Collections for a Genealogy of the Noble Families of
Henzy, Tyttery, and Tyzack . . . , by H. S. Grazebrook,
Stourbridge, 1877.

Hepburn—The Descent of the Hepburns of Monkrig, by J. A. Duncan, Edin., 1911 (50).
Genealogical Notes of the Hepburn Family, by Edward Hepburn, 4to, London, 1925.*

Herbert—The Herberts of Wilton, by Tresham Lever, 1967.

Heriot—Historical and Genealogical Notes . . . regarding the Family of Heriot of Trabroun, Edin., 1878.
Selections from old Records regarding the Heriots of Trabroun, by G. W. Ballingall, Haddington, 1894.
The Heriots of Ramornie, by R. C. Reid, Dumfries, 1931.

Heron—Genealogical and Historical Table of the Families of Heron . . . , by Sir Richard Heron, fo., London, 1797.*

Herrick—Some Early Notices of the Herrick Family, by the Rev. W. G. D. Fletcher, Leicester, 1885.

Herries—The Story and Pedigree of the Lords Herries, by C. H. Herries Crosbie, fo., wrapper, Wexford, 19—.

Hervey—An Account of the Parish of Ickford, and of the Family of Hervey, by Lord Arthur Hervey, ed. by J. J. Howard, 4to, Lowestoft, 1858.

Hesketh—The Genealogy of the . . . Family of the Heskaythes of Rufford . . . , 4to, London, 1869.*
Descent of the Hesketh of Kenwick, co. Salop, by Edwin Hobhouse, broadside, 1893.

Hett—A Family History . . . , by J. F. Hett, 1934.

Hewetson, Hewson—Memoirs of the House of Hewetson or Hewson of Ireland, by John Hewetson, London, 1901.
A Narrative of the Hewson and Bonsor Families, by Thomas

Hewson, 4to, Croydon, 1822.*

Heyden—The Heydens in England and America . . . , by the Rev.
W. B. Heyden, London, 1877.

Hicks, Hicks Beach—The Family of Hicks, by the Marquis of Ruvigny and Raineval, 4to, 1902 (100).
A Cotswold Family; Hicks and Hicks Beach, by Mrs William
Hicks Beach, london, 1909.

Higgins—The History of the Higgins and Burne Family, by R. V. H.
Burne, Manchester, 1925.*

Higginson—The Descendants of the Rev. Thomas Higginson, by
T. B. Higginson, London, 1958 (250).

Higgs—A History of the Higges or Higgs Family, by W. M. Higgs
and M. A. Higgs, Adlard, 1933.

Hill—A Genealogical Account of the Family of Hill of Court and
Alcaston, Shropshire, by the Rev. T. Leonard Hill, 1854;
revised and re-published by the Author, 4to, Bath, 1881.
The Early Records of an old Glasgow Family, by W. H. Hill,
Glasgow, 1902.*
An Account of the Julian Hill Family, by G. W. E. Hill, 1938.

Hilton—Short History of the Castle, Family and Estate of the
Hiltons of Hilton Castle, by the Rev. W. P. Swaby, Sunderland, 1884.

Hippisley—Some Notes on the Hippisley Family by A. E. Hippisley, ed. by I. Fitzroy Jones, Wessex Press, 1952.*

Hoare—Pedigrees and Memoirs of the Family of Hore . . . Hoare
. . . comp. by Sir Richard Colt Hoare, Bt., fo., Bath, 1819.*
Some Account of . . . the Families of Hore and Hoare, by Capt.

Edward Hoare of Cork, 4to, London, 1883.
History of my Family . . . , by J. N. Hoare, 1903.

Hobbs—Descendants of Charles Hobbs, 1596-1700, comp. by
F. M. Lupton, Leeds, 1914.

Hobhouse—Hobhouse Memoirs, by the Rt. Hon. Henry Hobhouse,
Wessex Press, 1927.*

Hodlestone—Famylie of Hodlestone of Salstone . . . , and of
Hodlestone, lords of Milham in the County of Cumber-
land, by John Taylor, London, 1641 (See N. and Q., 4th
Ser., III, 426.)

Hoggins—The Family of Hoggins of Great Boles, by the Rev.
W. G. D. Fletcher, paper, n.d.*

Holbrow—Some Account of the Family of Holbrow . . . , by
W. P. W. Phillimore, 4to, Devizes and London, 1901 (75).*

Holcroft—Notes on the Families of Holcroft . . . , by J. P.
Rylands, Leigh, 1877.*

Holden—The Derbyshire Holdens and their Descendants, by
W. H. Holden, 4to, (Apex Printing Service, W.C.), 1930
(100).*

Holland—A History of the Family of Holland of Mobberly . . .
From Materials collected by the late Edgar Swinton Holland,
ed. by William Ferguson Irvine, Edin., 1902.*
The Lancashire Hollands, by Bernard Holland, London, 1917.
Some Records of the Holland Family of Barton-under-Needwood,
by W. R. Holland, 1929.
See also Hallen.

Holt—A History of the Holtes of Aston, Baronets, by Alfred Davidson, fo., Birmingham, 1854.

Home, Hume–Genealogical Account of the Family of Home of
Wedderburn . . . , 4to, 10pp., 1776.
De Familia Humia Wedderburnensis, Liber I, by David Hume,
(before 1620); ed. by Dr John Miller for the Abbotsford
Club, 4to, Edin., 1839.
Marchmont and the Humes of Polwarth, by One of their
Descendants (Margaret Warrender), Edin., 1894.

Hood–The Admirals Hood, by Dorothy Hood, Hutchinson,
1941.

Hope–See Beresford Hope.

Hopkin–Hopkiniaid Morganwg, by Lemuel J. James, Bangor,
1909 (250).*

Hopkins–Genealogical Memoranda relating to the Families of
Hopkins . . . co. Mon., and Probyn of Newland, co. Glos.,
by J. A. Bradney, fo., London, 1889.

Hooker–The Hookers of Kew, by Mea Allan, 1967.

Horner–The Horner Family of Wakefield, co. York; Sheffield,
1879.

Hornyold–The Hornyold Family of Blackmore Park, co. Worcs.,
by T. C. G. Hornyold, 1883.

Horton–The Hortons of Howroyde, Yorks . . . , by E. F. Linton,
4to, Cambridge, 1911.
The Hortons of Leicestershire, by L. G. H. Horton-Smith,
1946.

Hotham–History and Cartulary of the Hothams of Scarborough

. . . , by Philip Saltmarshe, 4to, 1914.*

The Hothams; being the Chronicle of the Hothams of Scarborough and South Dalton, by A. M. W. Stirling, 2v., London, 1918.

Houblon—The Houblon Family . . . , by Lady Alice A. Houblon, 2v., London, 1907.

Houldsworth—The Beginnings of the Houldsworths of Coltness, by W. H. MacLeod and Sir H. H. Houldsworth, 4to, Glasgow, 1937.

Hovenden—Genealogical Memoranda relating to the Family of Hovenden, by R. Hovenden, Pt. I., 4to, wrapper, Taylor and Co., 1872.*

Lineage of the Family of Hovenden, Irish Branch, by R. Hovenden, 1892.*

Howard—Historical Anecdotes of Some of the Howard Family, by the Hon. Charles Howard, 12mo., London, 1769. (Suppressed by the author who as 10th Duke of Norfolk died 31. 8. 1786.); 2nd edn., 1817.

An Analysis of the Genealogical History of the Howard Family, by Sir T. C. Banks, London, 1812.

Genealogical History of the Noble House of Howard, London, 1830.

The Noble and Illustrious Family of Howard, by the Rev. Alfred Gatty, D.D., Sheffield, 1879.

The Howards of Effingham, by G. Leveson Gower, 1888.

The House of Howard, by G. Brenan and E. P. Statham, 2v., London, 1907.

The Lion and the Rose, Norfolk Line, 957-1646, Suffolk Line, 1603-1917, by Ethel M. Richardson, 2v., 1923.

The Howards of Norfolk, by Neil Grant, Watts, 1972.

Howe—By the Name of Howe; Facts and Dates, by Alfred Leighton Howe, wrapper, 1911.

Hubbard—Some Account of the Hubbard Family, by W. E. Hubbard, paper covers, Sevenoaks, 1917.

Hughes—The History of the Families of Hughes and Maunday . . . also some Facts of the Kitcat Family . . . revised by the Rev. David Kitcat and written out by G. M. P. Kitcat in 1900, London, 1908, and 4to, London, Ballantyne Press, 1913.

Hulton—Genealogy of the Family of Hulton of Hulton, co. Lancs., 48pp.*

Hume—See Home.

Hungerford—Hungerfordiana . . . collected by Sir R. Colt Hoare, Bt., Shaftsbury, 1823 (100).*

Hunter—Pedigree of Hunter of Abotshill and Barjarg, Hunter of Bonnington and Doonholm, Hunter-Blair of Blairquhan, Hunter of Auchterarder, and Hunter of Thurston, by Andrew A. Hunter, 4to, London, 1905.
Some Family Papers of Hunter of Hunterston . . . , by Gen. Hunter-Weston, Scottish Record Soc., 1925.

Hurry—Memorials of the Family of Hurry of Great Yarmouth . . . , by C. J. Palmer, 4to, Norwich, 1873 (150); 2nd edn., by Thomas Hurry-Houghton, 4to, Liverpool, C. Tinling and Co., 4to, 1926.

Hurt—The History of the Hurts of Holdsworth and their Descendants, by Sir George Sitwell, Bt., O.U.P., 1930.

Husey—A Brief Sketch of the Family of Husey . . . , 1867.*

Hutchinson—History of the Hutchinson Family from A.D. 1610
. . . , 4to, London, 1920.

Hutton—The Life of William Hutton, to which is subjoined the
History of the Family, by William Hutton 1798-9, published
by his daughter C. Hutton, London, 1816; 2nd edn., Birmingham and London, 1817; new edn., as one of Knight's English Miscellanies, 1841; French translation by E. Charton,
1864; re-issued, ed. by Llewellyn Jewitt, Chandos Library,
1872; a further edn. was issued, n.d.
Some Account of the Family of Hutton . . . , comp. by A. W.
Hutton, 4to, Devizes, 1898 (50).*
Supplementary Chapter and Index to the above, 'bringing the
record down to the end of the year 1902', 4to, wrapper, 1902.
Hutton Families, by J. A. and P. C. Hutton, 4to, 1939.

Huxley—The Huxleys, by R. W. Clark, Heinemann, 1968.

Hyland—The Family of Hyland, by T. A. Glenn, 1929.

I

I'Anson—The History of the I'Anson Family, by Bryan I'Anson,
fo., London, 1914.

Ingilby—The Early History of Ripley and the Ingilby Family . . .
with some account of the Roos Family of Ingmanthorpe, by
W. T. Lancaster, J. Whitehead and Son, Leeds and London,
4to, 1918 (40).

Inglis—Historical and Genealogical Notices of the Family of Inglis
of Milton Bryant, by C. H. Wilson, 4to, 1874.
The Family of Inglis of Auchendinny and Redhall, by J. A.
Inglis, 4to, Edin., 1904; 2nd edn., 1914.

Ingpen—An Ancient Family . . . , by A. R. Ingpen, 4to, Longmans, 1916.

Ingram–Sir Arthur Ingram, c. 1565-1642, A Study of the Origin
　　　of an English Landed Family, by Anthony F. Upton, n.d.

Innes–An Account of the Family of Innes, comp. by Duncan
　　　Forbes of Culloden, 1698, with an Appendix . . . , ed. by
　　　Cosmo Innes for the Spalding Club, 4to, 1864.
　　Historical Account of the Origine and Succession of the Fam-
　　　ily of Innes from the original MS. in the possession of the
　　　Duke of Roxburghe, ed. by Cosmo Innes, 4to, Edin., 1820.
　　The Castle and Lords of Balveny, by W. Cramond, LL.D.,
　　　Edin., 1893.
　　Chronicles of the Family of Innes of Edingight and Balveny,
　　　by Col. Thomas Innes of Loarney, 4to, Aberdeen, 1898.*
　　Notes on the Family of Innes of Newseat of Scurdargue, by
　　　A. N. Innes, London, 1931 (100).*

Intwood–The Intwood Story, by A. J. Nixseaman, Norwich, 1972.

Irby–The Irbys of Lincolnshire and the Irbys of Cumberland, by
　　　Paul A. Irby, 3v., 1938-9.

Ireland–Hale Hall with Notes on the Family of Ireland Blackburne,
　　　by Miss Blackburne of Hale Hall, 4to, Liverpool, 1881 (100).*

Irvine, Irving–The Original of the Family of the Irvines, by Dr
　　　Charles Irvine, 12mo., ? 1678.
　　A Short Account of the Family of Irvine of Drum . . . , by D.
　　　Wimberley, fo., Inverness, 1893.*
　　The Irvings, Irwins, Irvines, or Erinveines, by Col. J. B.
　　　Irving of Bonshaw, 4to, Aberdeen, 1907.
　　The Irvines of Drum and Collateral Branches, by Lt. Col.
　　　Jonathan Forbes Leslie, 4to, Aberdeen, 1909.*
　　The Irvings of Newton, by Miles Irving, 8pp., Aberdeen, 1909.
　　The Irvines of Drum, by R. Anderson, Peterhead, 1920.

Ivery–See Yvery.

J

Jacob—An Historical and Genealogical Narrative of the Family
of Jacob, including those who were Freeholders of the Man-
or of Haslingfield, co. Kent A.D. 1275 . . . , by A. A. Jacob
and J. H. Glascott, Dublin, 1875.*
A History of the Families of Jacob of Bridgewater, Tiverton,
and South Ireland, by H. W. Jacob, Taunton, Wessex Press,
1929.*

Jalland—Some Account of the Family of Jalland, originally of
Whatton in co. Notts, from 1535-1878, by John Jalland,
1849; 2nd edn., by H. G. Jalland, 58pp., Nottingham,
1878.

James—Genealogical Notes on the Descent of the Family of
James of Austin Friars, by Maj. Gen. E. R. James, 1898.*
Pedigrees of the Families of James of Culgarth, West Auckland
and Barrock . . . , comp. by H. E. M. J. and W. A. J., 4to,
Exeter, 1913 (additions and corrections, 4to, wrapper,
Exeter, 1914*).

Jeaffreson—Pedigree of the Jeaffreson Family with Notes and
Memoirs, by M. T. Jeaffreson, 4to, London, 1922 (50).

Jeffcock—Family Recollections, by W. P. Jeffcock, 1941.*

Jennens—The Great Jennens Case, being an Epitome of the History of the Jennens Family, comp. by Messrs. Harrison and
Willis, Sheffield, 1879.

Jephson—History of the Jephson Family, by Charlotte Fitzgerald,
4to, Bath, 1870.*

Jerrard—The Jerrard Family and its Chideock Branch, by F. B. J.
Jerrard, fo., 1912.

Jesper—Short History of the Jesper Family . . . , by W. A. Jesper, York, 1916.

Jodrell—Genealogical Memoranda relating to the Family of Jodrell, William Salt Soc., 1897.*

Johnson, Johnston—Genealogical Account of the Family of Johnston of that Ilk formerly of Caskieben . . . , by Alexander Johnston junr., 4to, Edin., 1832 (90).*
The Annandale Family Book of the Johnstones . . . , by Sir W. Fraser, 2v., 4to, Edin., 1894.
History of the Johnstones 1191-1909 . . . , by C. L. Johnstone, Edin., 1909; suppt., Glasgow, 1925.
The Johnsons of Maiden Lane, by Donald McDonald, Martins, 1964.

Joliffe—The Joliffes of Staffordshire and their Descendants, by H. G. H. Joliffe, 4to, London, 1892.

Josselyn—The Genealogical History of the Ancient Family of Josselyn, by J. H. Josselyn, 4to, Ipswich, 1880.

Judd—Thomas Judd and His Descendants, by Sylvester Judd, Northampton, 1856.

Jukes—A History of the Jukes Family of Cound, Shropshire (including other branches), by Percy W. L. Adams, Tunstall, 1927.*
See also Worthington.

Jupp—See Woodd.

K

Keating—Family Records and Recollections, by W. Keating, (F. J. Parsons), Bexhill-on-Sea, 1908.

Keddie—Three Generations: The Story of a Middle Class Scottish Family, by Henrietta Keddie (Sarah Tytler), London, 1911.

Keith—A Historical and Authentic Account of the Ancient and Noble Family of Keith, Earls Marshall of Scotland, by P. Buchan, 12mo., Peterhead, 1820.

Kemeys—The Family of Kemeys, by W. Kemmis, 1888.

Kemp—A General History of the Kempe Families . . . , by F. Hitchin-Kemp and Others, 4to, 1902; suppt. 1903.

Kendall—The Kendalls of Austrey, Twycross and Smithsby . . . , by H. J. B. Kendall, 4to, London, 1909.*

Kennedy—Historical and Genealogical Account of the Principal Families of the Name of Kennedy, ed. by R. Pitcairn, 4to, Edin., 1830.
   Historical Account of the Noble Family of Kennedy, Marquess of Ailsa and Earl of Cassilis, by David Cowan, 4to, Edin., 1849.
   A Family of Kennedy of Clogher and Londonderry, by Francis M. E. Kennedy, 1938.*

Kenrick—Chronicles of a Nonconformist Family (the Kenricks of Wynne Hall, Exeter and Birmingham), by Mrs W. Byng Kenrick, Birmingham, Cornish Bros., 1932 (deals also with Wynne).

Kenyon—Kenyon Family Biography, by R. L. C. Kenyon, pamph. 60pp., Shrewsbury, 1920.*

Kerneys—Sir Nicholas Kerneys . . . with the Family History and Pedigree, by J. Rowlands, 1881.

Ker, Kerr—Pedigree of the Family of Ker of Cessford, Greenhead,

and Prymsideloch, by Christian L. Reid, 4to, Newcastle, 1914.
Notices of the Family of Kerr of Kerrisland, by Robert Malcolm
Kerr, London, 1881 (25).

Kett—The Ketts of Norfolk, by L. M. Kett, Mitchell, Hughes, and
Clarke, 4to, 1921 (125).

Keyes—A Brief Notice of the late Thomas Keyes of West Boyl-
stone, together . . . with an Account . . . of His Descendants
. . . and of His Ancestors, 12mo., Worcester, 1857.

Kilner—The Descendants of James and Ann Kilner, formerly of
Mausegh, Westmorland, London, 1862.

Kincaid—Memorial of the Conversion of Jean Livingstone, 1600,
Edin., 1827, pp. 6-7.

Kinchant—Quienchant vel Quinchant vel Kinchant Family Notes,
by Maj.-Gen. J. Charlton Kinchant, 4to, London, 1917
(65).*

Kindersley—A History of the Kindersley Family, by A. F. Kindersley, 1938.*

King—Genealogies of the Families of Kings who lived in Raynham
from 1680 . . . , by E. Sanford, Taunton, 1866.
Genealogical Memoranda relating to the Family of King of Maid-
stone, by W. L. King, 4to, London, 1882.
Genealogical Record of the Families of King and Henham in
co. Kent, by W. L. King, 4to, London, 1899 (40).*
Memoir of the Family of Kings of Newmill, by R. Young, 1904.

King-Hall—Sea Saga, ed. by L. King-Hall, Gollancz, 1935.

Kingdon—The Kingdon Family, by F. B. Kingdon, Stanley Press,
1932.*

1932.*

A Second Look, by A. S. Kingdon, 1974.*

Kinloch—Kinloch of that Ilk . . . , by Eve T. Wayne, 1923.

Kinnaird—The Kinnairds of Culbin, by the Rev. J. G. Murray,
    Inverness, 1938.

Kircaldy—A Short History of the Family of Kircaldy of Grange,
    Monkwearmouth, and London, by James Kircaldy, 4to,
    London, 1903.*

Kirkland—See Bate.

Kirkpatrick—Memoir respecting the Family of Kirkpatrick of
    Closeburn, by Charles Fitzpatrick, 4to, London, 1858.
    Chronicles of the Kirkpatrick Family, by Alexander de
    Lapère Kirkpatrick, 4to, London, 1897.*

Kitcat—The House of Kitcat, by John Adams, G. and J. Kitcat,
    ? 1948.
    See also Hughes.

Knapp—A History of the Chief English Families bearing the name
    of Knapp, comp. by O. G. Knapp, 4to, London, 1911 (100).*

Knatchbull—Memoirs of the Family of Sir Edward Knatchbull
    . . . by R. Pocock, Gravesend, 1802.

Knill—Genealogy of the Knills of Knill, by J. L. Lambe, broad-
    side, 1902.

Knowles—Genealogy of the Knowles Family of Edgworth, Little
    Bolton, etc., by J. C. Scholes, 12mo., 1886 (50).*

Knox—Genealogy of the Knoxes of Kilbirnie, by William Logan,

4to, Kilmarnock, 1856.

Genealogical Memoirs of John Knox and the Family of
Knox, by the Rev. Charles Rogers, Grampian Club and
R. Hist. Soc., 1879.

Knox Genealogy: Descendants of William Knox and John
Knox the Reformer, by a Lineal Descendant (William Crawford), 4to, Edin., 1896 (120).

Andrew Knox, Bishop of Raphoe, and his Descendants,
Londonderry, 34pp., 1892.

Kynnersley—A History of the Family of Kynnersley of Leighton,
by T. F. Kynnersley, 1897.

L

Lacy—The Lacy Family in England and Normandy, by W. E.
Wightman, O.U.P., 1966.

Lamb—Some Annals of the Lambs, a Border Family, by Mabel
Lamb, 4to, Westminster Press, 1926.

Lambart, Lambert—Leaves from a Family Tree, by Edgar Lambart,
4to, London, Hatchard, 1902.*
Account of the Family of Lambert of Woodmansterne, Ban-
stead, etc., by A Surrey Antiquary (E. G.), 1886.

Lamont—An Inventory of Lamont Papers 1231-1897, ed. by Sir
Norman Lamont, Bt., Edin., 1914.
The Lamont Clan, by Hector McKechnie, 4to, Edin., 1938.

Lang—The Langs of Selkirk, by Patrick Sellar Lang, Melbourne,
1910.

Langdale—The Pedigree of the Langdale Family, comp. by W.
S. Langdale, London, 1873.

Langrish—The Family and Manor of Langrish, by Richard Langrish, 4to, Athlone, 11pp., ? 1885.

Langstaff—The Langstaffs of Teesdale and Weardale . . . , by George B. Langstaff, 4to, London, 1906-7; 2nd edn., 1919; 3rd edn., 1923.

Langton—Memorials of the Family of Langton of Kilkenny, by John G. A. Prinn, Dublin, 1884.
The Langtons of Langton in Lincolnshire, comp. by Charles Langton, Jersey, J. P. Bigwood, 4to, 1929-30 (100).

Lasham—Some Notes on the Family of Lasham of Hampshire, by Frank Lasham, sm. 4to., ? 1906.*

Lauder—The Lauders of the Bass and their Descendants, by C. A. B. Lawder, Belfast, 1914.

Launce—A Memorable Note: Wherein is Conteyned the Names in Part of the Chieftest Kindred of Robert Launce, late of Mettfield in Suffolk, deceased . . . , in facsimile by the Rev. S. B. Turner, fo., wrapper, 14pp., London, 1882.*

Laurie—A Family Memoir, by P. G. Laurie, Brentwood, 1901.
The Lauries of Maxwelton and other Laurie Families, by Isabel O. J. Gladstone, London, 1972.

Lavars—The Lavars Family of Cornwall, by John Lavars of Bristol, 1874.*

Lavington—The History of a Sussex Family, by Alan Wilberforce, 1919.*

Law—Lauriston Castle, the Estate and its Owners, by John A. Fairley, Edin., 1925.

Lawrance, Lawrence—A Branch of the Aberdeenshire Lawrances, by Robert Murdoch Lawrance, 4to, Aberdeen, 1925 (60).*
A Family History of the Lawrences of Cornwall, by Mrs Edith J. Durning-Lawrence, 1915.*

Laybourn—The House of Laybourn, by R. Laybourn, Copenhagen, 1938.

Lechmere—Hanley and the House of Lechmere, by E. P. Shirley, 4to, Chiswick Press, 1883.
The Lechmere Family, by J. W. Wood, 1890.

Leckie—Origin of the Name and Family of Leckie (Leckie of that Ilk), by R. G. E. Leckie, Vancouver, 1913.

Ledingham—Chronicles of a Historic Aberdeen Family, by A. Ledingham, Peterhead, 1924.

Lee—History and Pedigree of the Lee-Jortin Family, 1858.

Leech—The Leech Family of Ashton-under-Lyne, by E. B. Leech, 1924.

Legh, Leigh—History of the House of Lyme, by W. Beaumont, Warrington, 1876.
Genealogy of the Family of Lee, by the Rev. F. G. Lee, 1884.
Genealogical Memoir of the Extinct Family of Leigh of Addington, 1860, by H. S. A. Sweetmam, Torquay, 1887 (50).*
Memorials of a Warwickshire Family, by the Rev. B. G. F. C. W. Boughton-Leigh, O.U.P., 1906.
The House of Lyme . . . , by Lady Newton, 1917.

Leete—The Family of Leete with Special Reference to the Genealogy of Joseph Leete, by C. Bridger, ed. by J. C. Anderson, 4to, London, 1881;* 2nd edn., 4to, 1906.*

Leetham—The Origin and Lineage of the Leetham Family, by Lt. Col. Sir Arthur Leetham, 1919.

Leeves—A Family Memorial, by A. M. Moom, née Elsdale, of Brigton, 1872.

Le Fanu—Memoir of the Le Fanu Family, by T. P. Le Fanu, 1924 (150).

Lefroy—Notes and Documents relative to the Family of Leffroy . . . and Families of Lefroy, by a Cadet (J. Lefroy), fo., Woolwich, 1868.*

Legard—The Legards of Anlaby and Ganton . . . , by Sir J. Digby Legard, 1926.

Le Geyt—A Short Account of Le Geyt— dit Ranvet Family of St Saviours, Jersey, comp. by L. A. Bernau, 4to, 1906 (100).*

Leigh—See Legh.

Leighton—Memorials of the Leightons of Ulishaven, Angus, . . . A. D. 1260-1931, by Clarence F. Leighton, London, 1931.

Leith—The Leiths of Harthill, by Francis Bickley, Maclehose, 1937.

Le May—Records of the Le May Family . . . , by Reginald Le May, 1958.

Le Neve—The Le Neves of Norfolk, by Peter Le Neve-Foster, 1969 (200).

Lennard—An Account of the Families of Lennard and Barrett . . . , by T. Barrett-Lennard, 4to, 1908.*

Lenox-Cunningham—An Old Ulster House, by Mina Lenox-Cunningham, Dundalk, 1947.

Lenthal—Burford Priory and its Associations with the Lenthal Family, by Harry Painton, Oxford, 1907.

Leslie—Laurus Leslaeana Explicata . . . , by the Rev. William Lesly, S.J., fo., Gratz, 1667 and 1792.
Pedigree of the Family of Leslie of Balquhain . . . , by Col. Charles Leslie, 24pp., Bakewell, 1861.
Historical Records of the Family of Leslie from 1067 to 1869 . . . , by Col. C. Leslie of Balquhain, 3v. in 2, Edin., 1869; 3v. Aberdeen, 1880.
The Leslies of Tarbert . . . , by P. L. Pielou, Dublin, Brindleys, 1935.*
See also Melville.

Le Strange—Le Strange Records . . . , by Hamon Le Strange, 4to, London, 1916.

Lethbridge—The Lethbridges, a Devonshire Clan . . . , by Sir Roper Lethbridge (d. 1919).*

Lethieullier—The Lethieullier Family of Aldersbrook House, by C. H. I. Chown, 1927.

Levinge—History of the Levinge Family, by Sir R. Levinge, 4to, 1813.
Historical Notices of the Levinge Family, Ledestown, 1853.
Jottings for Early History of the Levinge Family, by Sir R. G. A. Levinge Bt., 4to, Dublin, 1873 (Pt I only published).

Lewen—History and Pedigrees of the Family of Lewen of Durham, Northumberland, and Scarborough . . . , by Sir T. E. Watson, 4to, 1919 (100).

Lightbody—Lightbody Record 1550-1930, by W. Lightbody, 1932.*

Limrick—The Family of Limrick, co. Cork, by the Rev. H. L. L. Denny, 8pp., 1909.

Lind—The Genealogy of the Family of Lind, by Sir Robert Douglas, Windsor, 1795.*

Lindsay—Lives of the Lindsays, A Memoir of the Houses of Crawford and Balcarres, by Lord Lindsay, 3v., or 4v. in 2, Wigan, 1840 (150 and 6 in 4to); 3v., London, 1849; and 3v., London, 1858.
The History and Traditions of the Land of the Lindsays . . . , by Andrew Jervise, Edin., 1853; 2nd edn., corrected by James Gammack, Edin., 1882.
The Lindesays of Loughry, by E. H. Godfrey, London, 1950
The Leafy Tree: my Family, by Sir E. D. L. Lindsay, Newnes, 1967.

Lingard—The Lingards of Huncoat . . . , by Richard Ainsworth, Harington, 1930.

Linley—The Linleys of Bath, by Clementina Black, London, 1911; 2nd edn. (Introduction by George Saintsbury), 1926; rev. edn., London, 1971.

Linton—See Horton.

Lisle, Lyle—The Lisles of Ellingham, by K. M. Briggs, Oxford, Alden Press, 1936.
De Insula or the Lyles of Renfrewshire, by William Lyle, Glasgow, 1936.*

Lister—Memorials of an Ancient House . . . , by the Rev. H. L. Lyster Denny, 4to, Edin., 1913 (250).

Little—The Family History, by E. Caruthers Little, 4to, Gloucester, 1892.*

Fragmentary Memories . . . an Account of the Clan Little . . . , ed. with others, by Robert Little, London, 1913.

Livingston—Notice Généalogique sur la Famille de Lévingston, ou Lavingston, ou Léviston, par M. le Maistre Tonnerre, 1856.

The Livingstons of Callender and their Principal Cadets, by E. B. Livingston, 4to, 5pts, in 2v., 1887-92 (75); 2nd edn., 4to, Edin 1920.

Lloyd—Farm and its Inhabitants, with some Account of the Lloyds of Dolobran, by Rachel J. Lowe, 4to, London, 1883.

The Lloyds of Birmingham, with some account of the founding of Lloyds Bank, by Samuel Lloyd, 1907, 2nd edn., Birmingham, 1907; 3rd edn., 1909.

Family Records of the Lloyds of Allt yr Odyn, by L. E. L. Theekston and J. Davies, 4to, Oxford, 1913.

The Quaker Lloyds . . . , by Humphrey Lloyd, Hutchinson, 1975.

Lobb—The Lobb Family, by G. Lobb-Eland, O.U.P., 1955.

Loch—The Family of Loch, by Gordon Loch (afterwards Dalyell), 4to, Constable, 1934 (100).

Lock—The Locks of Norbury, the Story of a Remarkable Family in the 18th and 19th centuries, by the Duchess of Sermoneta, 1940.

Lockett—Memoirs of the Family of Lockett, by R. C. Lockett, 1939.

Loftie—The Family of Loftie, by A. G. Loftie, Carlisle, 1918.*

Logan—The Logans of Knockshinnoch, 4to, Glasgow, 1869.

Hoc Majorum Virtus, (the same revised and corrected by
  J. M. H.), 4to, Edin., 1885.
History of the Logan Family, by Major G. J. N. Logan Home,
  4to, Edin., 1934.

Long–Historical Account of the Family of Long of Wiltshire, by
  Walter Chitty, London, 1889.
Records and Letters of the Family of the Longs of Longville,
  Jamaica, and Hampton Lodge, Surrey, ed. by R. M. How-
  ard, 2v., London, 1925.

Longsdon–Longsdon Family History, by E. H. Longsdon,
  Weybridge, 1967.

Loraine–Genealogy and other Memoirs . . . Loraine of Kirkharle
  Tower, by John White, Newcastle, 1738-40, reprinted
  1848 (100) as vol. 6 of Tracts printed by M. A. Richardson
  of Newcastle.
Pedigree and Memoirs of Loraine of Kirkharle, by Sir Lambton
  Loraine Bt., 4to, Westminster, Nicholls, 1902.*

Lovett–Ecclesiastical Memorials of the Lovett Family, by R. J.
  Arden Lovett, fo., Ostend, 1897.*

Lowe–Some Account of the Family of Lowe of Hartford (co.
  Chester), by A. W. Braunsdorff, Dresden, 1896.

Lowndes–A Cheshire Family, Lowndes of Overton, by W.
  Lowndes, Bures, 1972.

Lowther–Some Notes on the Lowthers . . . , in Ireland, . . .
  by Sir E. T. Bewley, Kendal, 1902.*

Lubbock–Notes on the History and Genealogy of the Family of
  Lubbock, by R. Birkbeck, 4to, 1891.*

Lucy—Biography of the Lucy Family of Charlecote Park, by M. E. Lucy, 4to, London, 1862.
Charlecote and the Lucys, by A. Fairfax-Lucy, O.U.P., 1958.

Lukin—Melusine and the Lukin Family, by Sir A. Tudor-Craig, 4to, The Century House, 1932 (125).*

Lumley—Records of the Lumleys of Lumley Castle, by E. Milner, ed. by E. Benham, 4to, London, 1904.
The Ancient Northern Family of Lumley and its Northampton-shire Branch, by L. G. H. Horton-Smith, St Albans, 1948.
The Late Lumleys of Harlestone, by L. G. H. Horton-Smith, Northampton, 1944.

Lumsden—Memorials of the Families of Lumsdaine, Lumisden, or Lumsden, by Lt. Col. H. W. Lumsden, R.A., 4to, Edin., 1889 (80).

Luttrell—A Genealogical Account of the Family of Lutrell, Lott-erell; or Luttrell, 4to, Milborne Port, 1774.*
See also Mohun.

Luvel—See Yvery.

Luxmoore—The Family of Luxmoore, by C. F. C. Luxmoore, Exeter, c. 1935.

Lyde—Lyde Records, by F. L. Caunter, 1933.*

Lyle—See Lisle.

Lynch—Notices Historiques sur quelques membres de la famille de Lynch, Paris, 1842.
Genealogical Memoranda relating to the Lynch Family of Kent . . . , 4to, London, 1883.

Lyon–Lyon of Ogil . . . , by William Lyon, 10th of Ogil, London, Field and Turner, c. 1869.

The Lyons of Cossins and Wester Ogil, cadets of Glamis, by Andrew Ross, 4to, Edin., 1901.

See also Bowes-Lyon.

Lyons–Historical Notice . . . of the Family of Lyons (Ireland), 26pp., Ledestown, 1853.

Lyte–Notices of the Lyte Family of Lytes Cary Manor House, by William George, Bristol, 4to, 1879 (30).

The Lytes of Lytes Cary, by Henry Maxwell Lyte, Taunton, 1895.

Lyttleton–The Genealogy of the Littleton Family, by W. F. Carter, Exeter, n.d.

M

Macauley–Aulay: Memoirs of Clan Aulay . . . , by a Sister of T. B. Macaulay, Carmarthen, 4to, 1881.*

Ardincaple and its Lairds, by E. R. Welles, Glasgow, Jackson Wylie, 1930.

McCall–Memoirs of my Ancestors . . . , by H. B. McCall, 4to, Birmingham, 1884 (150).

MacCarthy–A Historical Pedigree of the Sliochd Feidhlimidh, the MacCarthys . . . , by Daniel MacCarthy, Exeter, 1880.*

The MacCarthys of Munster, by S. T. MacCarthy, 1922.

M'Combie–Memoir of the Family of M'Combie . . . , by William M'Combie Smith, Edin., 1887; 2nd edn., as Memoir of the Families of M'Combie and Thoms . . . Edin. and London, 1890.

The McCombies of Dalkirby, by Mrs E. McCombie Fenn

1953.

MacConnel—Facts and Traditions collected for a Family Record,
by D. C. MacConnel, 4to, Edin., 1861.*

MacCorquodale—The Barons of Phantilands, or the MacCorquodales
and their Story, by Peter Macintyre, n.d.

MacCrimmon—The MacCrimmons of Skye . . . , by Fred T. MacLeod
Edin., 1933.
The MacCrimmon Family 1500-1936, by G. C. B. Poulter and
C. P. Fisher, Camberley, 1936.
A History of the Clan MacCrimmon, comp. by G. C. B. Poulter
(Clan MacCrimmon Soc.), 2pts., 1938-9.

Macdonald—A Keppoch Song, being the Origin and History of the
Family, by John P. Macdonald, Montrose, 1815.
Historical and Genealogical Account of the Clan . . . , by
Hector Macdonald Buchanan, 2pts., Edin., 1819.
Vindication of the Clanranald of Glengarry . . . , by John Rid-
del, Edin., 1821.
Genealogical and Historical Account of the Clan or Family of
Macdonald of Sandra, London, 1825.
Sketch of the History of the Macdonalds of the Isles, by
Alexander Sinclair, Edin., 1858.
Macdonald Family Genealogy to 1876, oblong, 1871.
History of the Macdonalds of Clanranald, by Alexander Mac-
Kenzie, 4to, Inverness, 1881 (150).
Family Memoir of the Macdonalds of Keppoch, by Angus
Macdonald, M.D., ed. by C. R. Markham, London, 1885.*
Moidart, or among the Clanranalds, by the Rev. Charles Mac-
donald, Oban, 1889.
The Last Macdonalds of Isla . . . , from Documents in the
Possession of Charles Fraser-Mackintosh, 4to, Glasgow, 1895.
The Clan Macdonald, by the Rev. A. J. and the Rev. A. M. Mac-
donald, 3v., 4to, Inverness, 1896-1904 (150 on large paper).

A Romantic Chapter in the Family History, by Alice Bosville
  Macdonald of the Isles, London, 1911.
Macdonalds of the Isles, by A. M. W. Stirling, London, John
  Murray, 1913.
The House of the Isles, by Lady (A. E. M.) Macdonald of the
  Isles, Edin., 1925.
Annals of the Macdonald Family, by Edith Macdonald, Horace
  Marshall and Son, 1928.

MacDonnell–The MacDonnells of Antrim, by the Rev. George Hill,
  4to, Belfast and London, 1873 and 1874.

MacDuff–Memorials of the Family of MacDuff, by – Ravenscroft,
  Aberdeen, 1948.
The Book of Colonsay and Oronsay, by Symington Grieve,
  Edin., 1923.

MacEwen–Clan Ewan, Some Records of its History, by R. S. T.
  MacEwen, Glasgow, 1904 (300).

MacFarlane–History of the Clan Macfarlane, by James Mac-
  Farlane, Glasgow, 1922.

MacGillicuddy–The MacGillicuddy Papers, by W. M. Brady, 4to,
  London, 1867.

MacGregor–Historical Notices of the Clan Gregor, by Donald
  Gregory, 4to, Pt I. only published, Edin., 1831.
Historical Memoirs of Rob Roy and the Clan MacGregor, by
  K. Macleay, Glasgow, 1818; 2nd edn. 1819; 3rd edn.,
  Edin., 1881.
Short Account of the Family of Gregor from the time they
  gave up the name of MacGregor, by Georgina Gregory,
  1873.
History of the Clan Gregor . . . , by A. G. M. MacGregor, 4to,
  2v., Edin., 1898-1901 (20 copies on van Gelder paper).

The Clan MacGregor . . . the nameless clan, by W. R. Kermack, Edin., 1953.

MacIntyre—The MacIntyres of Glencoe and Camus-na-h-erie, by Duncan Macintyre, Edin., 1901.

MacIver—Account of the Clan Iver, by the Very Rev. P. C. Campbell, Aberdeen, 1868, 1873 (150), 1878, with later issues.

Mackay—History of the House and Clan of Mackay . . . , by Robert Mackay, Thurso, 4to, Edin., 1829.*
Genealogy of the Family of Mackay, sometime of Sandwood, parish of Kinlochbervie . . . , by Angus Mackay, ed. by W. P. W. Phillimore, London, 1904.
The Book of Mackay, by Angus Mackay, 4to, Edin. and Wick, 1900 (500) (also published in Canada).
The Men from whom we have come; a Short History of the Mackays of Achmonie, Inverness, 1925.

McKee—The Book of McKee, by R. W. McKee, Dublin, 1959 (500).

Mackenzie—The Genealogy of the Mackenzies preceeding Ye Year 1661, by A Persone of Quality (Mackenzie of Applecross), 1669, ed. by J. W. Mackenzie, 4to, Edin., 1829 (50); also Dingwall, 4to, 1843.
The Genealogie of the Most Considerable Families descended of the Males of the House of Mackenzie, preceeding the year 1667, 4to, 1830 (sometimes bound with the preceeding).
The Earls of Cromartie . . . , by Sir William Fraser, 4to, 2v., Edin., 1876-7.
Some Account of the M'Kenzies of Finegand in Glenshee, Blairgowrie, 1889.*
The History of the Clan MacKenzie, by Alexander Mackenzie, 4to, Inverness, 1879, republished 1894.
The Genealogy of the Stem of the Family of Mackenzie

(Lords Seaforth), by E. M. Mackenzie (formerly Thompson), Melbourne, 1904.

The Mackenzies of Ballone, by H. H. Mackenzie, Inverness, 1941.

McKenna—Origin . . . with a History of the Sept, by Anthony Mathews, Dublin, 1872.

MacKinnon—Genealogical Account of the Family of MacKinnon, by Sir A. M. Downie and A. D. MacKinnon, 4to, Plymouth, 1882; 2nd edn., by Lauchlan MacKinnon, 14pp., London, 1883.

Memoirs of Clan Fingon . . . , by the Rev. Donald D. Mackinnon, Tunbridge Wells, 1884-6; 2nd edn., 1899.*

The Clan MacKinnon, by C. R. Mackinnon, Coupar Angus, 1958.

Mackintosh—Historical Memoirs of the House and Clan of Macintosh and of the Clan Chattan, by A. M. Shaw, 4to, London, 2v., 1880 (50); 2nd edn., Edin., 1903 (250 8vo, and 25 4to copies).

Account of the Confederation of the Clan Chattan, by Charles Fraser-Mackintosh, 4to, Glasgow, 1898.

Mackintosh Families in Glenshee and Glen Isla, by A. M. Mackintosh, Nairn, 1916.

The Clan Mackintosh and the Clan Chattan, by Margaret Mackintosh, Edin., 1948.

McLachlan—Records of a Family, by H. McLachlan, 1935.
See also Campbell-Maclachlan.

MacLagan—The Clan of the Bell of St Fillan, by R. C. Maclagan, M.D., Edin., 1879.

MacLagan Families, by Sir E. D. MacLagan, 4to, Edin. U. P., 1936.

MacLaren–The MacLarens . . . , by Margaret MacLaren, Aeneas
Mackay, 1960.

MacLaurin–History in Memoriam of the Clan Laurin . . . , by
Daniel MacLaurin, London, c. 1867.

MacLean–Historical and Genealogical Account of the Clan of
Maclean . . . , by a Seneachie (John Campbell Sinclair),
London and Edin., 1838.
History of Clan Tarlach o'Bui, by Lt. Col. Charles M.
M'Lean, Aberdeen, 1865.
Brief Genealogical Account of the Family of M'Lean, by
Alexander M'Lean, Edin., 1872.*
The Macleans of Boreray, by H. H. McKenzie, Inverness,
1946.
Clan Gillean, by J. N. M. MacLean, London, 1854.

MacLellan–Record of the House of Kirkcudbright, written by
John McClellan, Castle Douglas, 1874; 2nd edn., revd. by
G. P. MacClellan, Dumfries, 1906.

Macleod–History of the Macleods . . . , by Alexander Mackenzie,
Edin., 1888; Inverness, 1889 (100).
The MacLeods; a Short Sketch . . . , by the Rev. R. C. Macleod,
Edin., 1906.
History of the Macleods of Dunvegan and Lewis, 463pp.,
Inverness, 18–.
The MacLeods of Dunvegan, by the Rev. Canon R. C. Mac-
leod of Macleod, Clan Macleod Soc., 1927;* abridged
edn., 1929.
The Macleods of Arnisdale, by the Rev. D. Mackinnon, 4to,
Dingwall, 1929.
The Macleods, their Chiefs and Cadets, by Donald MacKinnon,
Cupar Fife, 1950.
The History of a Clan, by J. F. Grant, Faber, 1959.
The MacLeods–the Genealogy of a Clan, by D. MacKinnon

and A. Morrison, Edin., in parts 1969—.

MacLysaght—Short Study of a Transplanted Family . . . , by E. MacLysaght, Dublin, 1935.

MacManus—See Sotheron.

MacMillan—The House of MacMillan, by Charles Morgan, London, 1943.
The MacMillans and Their Septs, by the Rev. Somerled MacMillan, Glasgow, 1952.

MacNab—The Clan MacNab . . . , by John M'Nab, Clan MacNab Assn., Edin., 1907.
A Brief Outline of the Story of the Clan McNab, by A. C. McNab, Glasgow, 1951.

Macnachtan—Chiefs of Clan Macnachtan and Their Descendants, by Angus I. Macnachtan, Windsor, 1951.

Macnamara—The Story of an Irish Sept, by N. C. Macnamara, 1896.

MacNish—The History of the Clan Neish or MacNish, by David McNish and W. A. Tod, Edin., Blackwood, 1925.

Macpherson—The Chiefs of the Clan Macpherson, by W. Cheyne-Macpherson, Edin., 1947.

MacRae—Genealogical Account of the MacRaes, by the Rev. John MacRa, minister of Dingwall, 1704; Scottish Hist. Soc. 2nd ser., 5, V (1914).
History of the Clan Macrae . . . , by the Rev. Alexander Macrae, Dingwall, 1899, 1908, and 4to, 1910.

Madan—The Madan Family and the Maddens in Ireland and England, by Falconer Madan, O.U.P., 1933.

Maddison—A History of the Maddison Family (Lincs and Ireland), by Canon A. R. Maddison, Lincoln, 1910 (25).*

Mainwaring—A Short History of the Mainwaring Family, by R. M. Finley, London, 1890.*
The Mainwarings of Whitmore and Biddulph . . . , ed. by J. G. Cavenagh-Mainwaring, William Salt Soc., 1934.

Maitland—A Short Genealogy of the Family of Maitland, Earl of Lauderdale, by Prof. Andrew Dalzel, 4to, Edin., 1785, 1868, and 1875.
Genealogical and Historical Account of the Maitland Family . . . , by G. H. Roger Harrison, Windsor Herald, 4to, London, 1860 and 1869.

Major—Some Account of the Families of Major and Henniker, by J. H. Major, 4to, London, 1803.

Malet—Notices of an English Branch of the Malet Family, by Arthur Mallet, sm. 4to, London, 1885.*

Malim—The Malim Family, by the Rev. Alfred Malim, 4to, 55pp., c. 1897.

Malthus—Collections for a History of the Family of Malthus, by J. O. Payne, 4to, London, 1890 (110).*

Mann—Genealogy of the Mann Family, by the Rev. J. Mann, 1873.

Mansel—See Maunsell.

Marcroft—The Marcroft Family, by W. Marcroft, Manchester, Heywood and Co., 1886.*

Mark—Genealogy of the Family of Mark or Marke . . . , by J.
   Yarker, 4to, Manchester, 1898.*

Markham—A History of the Markham Family, by the Rev. David
   F. Markham, London, 1854; 2nd edn., entitled Markham
   Memorials, by Sir Clements R. Markham, 4to, 2v., London,
   1913.
   Genealogy or Petigree of Markham; finished at ye Charges
   and Prayers of Francis Markham, 1611, ed. by C. R. Mark-
   ham, 2pts., London, 1872.
   History of the Markhams of Northamptonshire, by C. A.
   Markham, Northampton, 1890 (100).*

Marley—The Marleys of Langton . . . , by Thomas W. Marley, 4to,
   wrapper, n.d.; 2nd edn., 1921.

Marmyun—History of the Ancient Noble Family of Marmyun . . . ,
   by Sir T. C. Banks, 8vo, and 4to, London, 1817.
   History of the Baronial Family of Marmion, Lords of the
   Castle of Tamworth, by C. F. R. Palmer, Tamworth and
   London, 1875.
   See also Dymock.

Marsden—Genealogical Memoirs of the Family of Marsden . . . , by
   B. J. J. A. and R. S. Marsden, 4to, wrappers, Birkenhead,
   1914.*

Marshall—Miscellanea Marescalliana, by George W. Marshall, 2v.,
   London, 1883-8 (51).*

Marsham—Registers of the Marshams of Kent . . . , by the Hon. R.
   Marsham-Townsend, 2v., fo., London, 1903-8.

Martin, Martyn—The Martins of Skye; a Short History of a Highland Family . . . , Glasgow, n.d.
   Genealogical Memoranda relating to the Family of Martyn, by

M. Williams, 4to, London, 1873.*
The Genealogy of the Martins of Ross, by S. Clarke, 1910.
The House of Martin . . . , by W. G. W. Watson, Exeter, 1906.
History of the Martin Family, by Stapleton Martin, 1909;*
2nd edn. 1916.
The History of the Martyn or Martin Family, by Bryan
I'Anson, Pt. 1, 4to, 1915 (250).

Martineau—Notes on the Pedigree of the Martineau Family descended from Gaston Martineau, who emigrated to England
in 1686, by David Martineau, 4to, London, 1907 (with
additions and notes 1909).*

Maskelyne—Notes on the Maskelyne Family and their Home, by
Mrs Story Maskelyne, Devizes, Woodward, 1916.

Mascy—The Descent of the Mascys of Rixton, by Mrs A. Tempest,
1889.

Massy—A Genealogical Account of the Massy Family, Dublin, 1890.

Master—Some Notices of the Family of Master . . . , by the Rev.
G. S. Master, London, 1874* (Soc. Gen. has typescript
addendum, c. 1929).

Masterman—The Pedigree of the Masterman Family, by C. R.
Everett, 4to, Newcastle, 1914.

Matheson—History of the Mathesons . . . , by Alexander Mackenzie, Inverness, 1882; 2nd edn., by Alexander MacBain,
Stirling and London, 1900 (500).

Maude—History of the Ancestors and Descendants of Sir Robert
Maude 1676-1750, comp. by Capt. F. Maude, 1886.*
Record of the Maude Family . . . , by Col. E. Maude, 12mo.,
1901.

The Maude Family . . . a Table based on information collected
   by the Hon. Francis Maude, R.N., introduction by
   Blanche Lyster, 2nd edn., 4to, 1903.*

Maugham—Somerset and all the Maughams, by Robin, 2nd
   Viscount Maugham, Heinemann, 1966.

Maule—Registrum de Panmure . . . , comp. by the Hon. Harry
   Maule of Kelly, 1733, ed. by John Stuart, 2v., 4to, Edin.,
   1874.*
   The Panmure Papers . . . , ed. by Sir D. Douglas and Sir G. D.
   Ramsay, 2v., 1908.
   History of the Maules, ed. by G. E. Maule, Folkestone, 1914.*

Maunday—See Hughes.

Maunsell, Mansel—An Historical and Genealogical Account of the
   Family of Maunsell, Mansell, or Mansel, by W. W. Mansel,
   Pt. 1. only, 4to, 88pp., London, 1850.*
   Poetical History of the Family of Maunsell, with notes by
   George Baker, wrapper, 1867.
   History of Maunsell or Mansell . . . , by R. G. Maunsell, 4to,
   Cork, 1903.
   History of the Family of Maunsell, from data collected by Col.
   C. A. Maunsell, written by F. P. Statham, 4to, 2v. in 3,
   1917-20.

Maxtone—The Maxtones of Cultoquhey, by E. Maxtone Graham,
   Edin., 1935.

Maxwell—Memoirs of the Maxwells of Pollok, by Sir William
   Fraser, 4to, 2v., Edin., 1863 (150).*
   The Book of the Caerlaverock; Memoirs of the Maxwells
   Earls of Nithsdale . . . , by Sir William Fraser, 4to, 2v.,
   Edin., 1873 (150).
   Records of the Maxwells of Bredieland, Marksworth, Castle-

head . . . , 8vo, n.d.
The Story and Pedigree of the Lords Herries . . . , by C. H.
Herries-Crosbie, wrapper, fo., Wexford, 19—.

May—The Mays of Basingstoke, by F. Ray, 4to, London, 1904.

Mayo—A Genealogical Account of the Mayo and Elton Families
of the Counties of Wilts and Hereford . . . , by the Rev.
C. H. Mayo, 4to, Chiswick Press, 1882; 1885; and 4to,
1908 (250).*

Meeson—A Genealogical Record of the Family of Meeson, by F.
Meeson, 1906-11; another edn., 1915-16.

Mellard—The Mellards; their Descendants . . . , by A. L. Reade,
4to, London, 1915* (includes an account of the Bibbys
of Liverpool).

Melville—The Melvilles, Earls of Melville, and the Leslies,
Earls of Leven, by Sir William Fraser, 4to, 3v., Edin., 1890
(150).*
The Melville Family . . . , by E. S. Joubert de la Ferté, 4to,
1920.

Menzies—The Red and White Book of Menzies, by D. P. Menzies,
4to, Glasgow, 1894; 2nd edn., Plean, 1908.*
The Red and White Book of Menzies . . . , a Review, by C.
Poyntz Stewart, Exeter, 1906 (reprinted from 'The
Genealogist').
The Lanark Manse Family . . . , by E. B. Menzies, ed. by Thom-
as Reid, 4to, Lanark, 1901.

Mercer—The Mercer Chronicle, by An Irish Sennachie, London,
1866.
Our Seven Centuries . . . , by G. R. Mercer, 4to, Perth, 1868.
The Mercers, by R. S. Fittis, Perth, 1877.

Meriet—Genealogy of the Somersetshire Family of Meriet, by B. W. Greenfield, Taunton, 1883.

Merivale—Family Memorials, by Anna W. Merivale, Exeter, 1864.*

Merriam—Genealogical Memoranda relating to the Family of Merriam, by C. P. Merriam and C. E. Gildersone-Dickinson, 4to, Chiswick Press, 1900 (112).

Merriman—Pedigree of the Family of Merriman and Notes . . . , by G. F. M. Merriman, London, 1918 (twelve on large paper).*

Mervyn—Fasciculus Mervinensis . . . , by Sir W. R. Drake, fo., London, 1873.*

Metcalfe—Records of the Family of Metcalfe, formerly of Nappa in Wensleydale, arrd. by W. C. and G. Metcalfe, London, 1891 (50).*
Family Notes and Reminiscences, by Mary A. Metcalfe-Gibson, 1899.
Medecalf, by the Rev. Thomas Metcalf, Beccles, William Clowes, 1930.*

Methold—Pedigree of the Methwold Family, now called Methold, from 1180-1870, by Some Members of the Family, 4to, London, 1870.*

Middlemore—Some Account of the Family of Middlemore of Warwickshire and Worcestershire, by W. P. W. Phillimore and W. F. Carter, 4to, London, 1901;* supplement, 1903-4.

Middleton, Myddleton—The Earls of Middleton . . . and the Middleton Family, by A. C. Biscoe, London, 1876 (creation of 1656).
Notes on the Middleton Family of Denbighshire and London,

by W. D. Pink, Chester, 1891 (100).*
Pedigree of the Family of Myddleton of Gwaynyog . . . , attempted by W. M. Myddleton, 4to, Horncastle, 1910.

Mieville—The Family of Mieville, by Sir W. F. Mieville, 4to, 1902.*

Mildmay—Genealogical Memoranda relating to the Family of Mildmay, comp. by J. J. Howard, 4to, wrapper, London, 1871.*
A Brief Memoir of the Mildmay Family, by H. St J. Mildmay, 1913.*

Miller—Memorials of Hope Park . . . , by W. F. Miller, 4to, 1856 (50).*
The Millers of Haddington, Dunbar, and Dunfermline, by W. J. Couper, London, 1914.
Some Account of the Miller Family of Ramsgate, by W. H. Higgs, 1939.

Minet—Some Account of the Huguenot Family of Minet . . . , by William Minet, 4to, London, 1892 (250).*

Minto—See Elliot.

Moffat—Short History of the Family of Moffat of that Ilk, by Robert Maxwell Moffat, M.D., 4to, Jersey, 1908.*

Mohun—Dunster and its Lords 1066-1881, by Sir H. C. Maxwell Lyte, Exeter, 1882 (200).*
History of Dunster and the Families of Mohun and Luttrell, by Sir H. C. Maxwell Lyte, 2v., London, 1909.

Moir—See Byres.

Molineux—Account of the Family and Descendants of Sir Thomas

Molyneux, by Sir Capel Molyneux Bt., n.d.; reprinted by
Sir Thomas Phillipps, 12mo., and 4to, Evesham, 1820-1
(50).

Memoir of the Molineux Family, by Gisborne Molineux, 4to,
London, 1882.*

Monckton—Genealogical History of the Family of Monckton, by
D. H. Monckton, 4to, London, 1887 (105).*

Moncrieff, Moncreiffe—The House of Moncrieff, by George Seton,
4to, Edin., 1890 (150).*

Our Forefathers, by Mary Anne Scott Moncreiff, 4to, 1895.*

The Moncrieffs and the Moncreiffes, by Frederick Moncrieff
and William Moncreiffe, 2v., 4to, Edin., 1929 (150).*

Monoux—Original Documents relating to the Monoux Family, by
G. F. Bosworth and C. D. Saunders, 4to, Walthamstow Antiq.
Soc., 1928.

Monro, Munro—The Monros of Auchinbowie and Cognate Families, by John A. Inglis, 4to, Edin., 1911-12.*

An Account of some Remarkable Particulars concerning the
Ancient Family of the Munros of Foulis, by P. Doddridge,
D.D., 28pp., London, 1747, 1753, 1814, and 1894.

History of the Munros of Foulis . . . , by Alexander Mackenzie,
Inverness, 1898.

Fowlis Castle and the Munroes of Lower Iveagh, by Canon
Horace Monroe, Mitchell Hughes and Clarke, 1929.

Montagu—Cowdray, the History of a Great English House, by
Mrs Charles Roundell, 4to, London, 1884.

The Montagus of Boughton and their Northamptonshire
Homes . . . , by C. Wise, Kettering, 1888.

Hinchinbroke . . . , by E. G. H. Montagu, London, 4to, 1910.

Montfort—History of the de Montfort Family, by J. D. White, 1894.

Montgomerie, Montgomery—Memorables of the Montgomeries
. . . (17th century rhyme), 4to, Glasgow, Foulis, 1770; reprinted Edin., 1822 (70).

Genealogy of the Montgomeries of Smithton, by Sir Robert
Douglas, Bt., Windsor, 1795.

A Genealogical History of the Family of Montgomery, by
E. G. S. Reilly, 4to, 88pp., wrappers, 1839-42.*

Memorials of the Montgomeries, Earls of Eglinton, by Sir
William Fraser, 4to, 2v., Edin., 1859.*

A Genealogical Account of the Family of Montgomeries of
Brigend of Don, by William Anderson, 4to, Edin., 1859.

Historical Memoir of the Family of Eglinton and Winton, by
John Fullarton, Ardrossan, 1864.

Généalogie de Montgomery; Ecosse, Etats Unis, France,
Comtes d'Eglintoun, Seigneurs de Greenfield. . . , fo., n.d.

A History of Montgomery of Ballyleck, by G. S. Montgomery,
1891.

Origin and History of the Montgomerys, by B. G. de Montgomery, Blackwood, 1948.

A General History of the Families of Montgomery of Garboldisham,
and Montgomerie of Fittleworth, by C. A. H. Franklyn, 1968.*

Montmorency—Histoire Généalogique de la Maison de Montmorency, by André du Chesne, Paris, 1624.

A Genealogical Memoir of the Family of Montmorency, by
Henry de Montmorency-Morres, 4to, Paris, 1817.

Les Montmorency de France et les Montmorency d'Irlande,
Précis Historique, par le Col. H. de Montmorency, 4to,
Paris, 1828 (see Round, Peerage and Family History, 20).

Moodie, Mudie—The Moodie Book . . . , by the Marquis de Ruvigny et Raineval, 4to, London, 1906 (150).*

The Moodies of Melsetter, by E. H. Burrows, Cape Town, 1954.

The Mudies of Angus, by Sir R. F. Mudie and Ian M. N. Mudie,
Broughty-Ferry, 1959.

Moor, More—The Family of de la Moor . . . Moor de Moorehayes
. . . , by the Rev. Cecil Moore, Pt. 1, 4to, London, 1884.*
History of the More Family . . . , by G. D. F. and C. C. More,
Birmingham, 1893.
The Family of Moore, by the Countess of Drogheda, Belfast,
1902, 4to, and Dublin, 1906.
Erminois, a Book of Family Records, by the Rev. C. Moor,
D.D., 4to, Kendal, 1918.
The Moores of Moore Hall, by J. Hone, 1939.

Mordaunt—The Mordaunts, by Lady (Elizabeth) Hamilton, Heinemann, 1965.

Morgan—Historical and Genealogical Memoirs of the Morgan Family, by G. Blacker Morgan, 4to, 2v., 1890-1.*

Morris—Morris of Ballybeggan and Castle Morris, by the Marquis
of Ruvigny et Raineval, 4to, 1904.*
Memoirs of My Family . . . , by Mrs E. Naomi Chapman, Butler
and Tanner, 1928.*
The Morris Family of South Molton, by R. B. Morris, 1908.

Morrison—The Clan Morrison, by Nancy B. Morrison, Glasgow,
1951.
The Clan Morrison, by Alick Morrison, Edin., 1956.

Morton—The Stem of Morton . . . , comp. by W. Morton, London,
1895.*
Vestigia Mortoni, 3pts, 8vo, wrapper, (all printed), 156pp.,
1886-7.

Mosley—Family Memoirs, by Sir Oswald Mosley, 4to, 1849.*
Moseley Family Memoranda . . . , ed. by E. Axon, 4to, Chetham
Soc., 1902.

Moss—The Staffordshire Family of Moss, by A. W. Moss, Walsall,

1937.

Mostyn—History of the Family of Mostyn, by Lord Mostyn and T. A. Glenn, 1925 (154).*

Moule—Elmley Lovett and the Moules of Sneads Green, by Canon Horace Monroe, 1927.
The Family of Moule of Melksham, Fordington and Melbourn, comp. by the Rev. W. M. Lewis, 1928.*

Moutray—Moutray of Seafield and Roscobie, now of Favour Royal, co. Tyrone, by the Marquis of Ruvigny et Raineval, 4to, London, 1902.

Mudge—Mudge Memoirs . . . , ed. by S. R. Flint, 4to, Truro, 1883, (100).

Mudie—See Moodie.

Muirhead—Account of the Family of Muirhead of Lachop . . . , by Walter Grosett of Logie, 18—.

Mulock—The Family of Mulock, by Sir E. T. Bewley, 4to, Dublin, 1905.*

Munro—See Monro.

Murchison—Family Notes and Reminiscences, by Sir K. Murchison, 1940.*

Mure—The History and Descent of the House of Rowallane, by Sir William Mure of Rowallane (written 1657 or before), with preface by William Muir, 12mo., Glasgow, 1825; another edn., 1898.

Muriel—A Fenland Family . . . , by J. H. L. Muriel, 1968.

Murray—The Murrays of Blackbarony, by Sir Digby Murray, Bt.,
1891.

The Murrays of Ochertyre, by Albert D. Kippen, Crieff, 1893.

Chronicles of Atholl and Tullibardine Families, ed. by John, 7th
Duke of Atholl, 5v., Edin., 1908.

The Murrays of Elibank, by A. C. Murray, Edin., 1917.

Musgrave—Collectanea Musgraviana, by Percy Musgrave, 4to, Leeds,
1911.*

Mushet—The Story of the Mushets (of Dalkeith), by F. M. Osborn,
London, 1952.

Myddleton—See Middleton.

Mylne—The Mylne Family, by R. W. Mylne, 4to, 1877.

The Master Masons of Scotland . . . , by the Rev. Robert Scott
Mylne, Edin., 1893.

N

Napier—Memoirs of John Napier of Merchiston, his Lineage . . . ,
by Mark Napier, 4to, Edin., and London, 1834.

Some Notes on the Napiers of Merchiston and Scotts of Thirl-
stane, by Francis Lord Napier, paper covers, n.d.

Nugae Antiquae. Genealogical Notes of the Napiers of Kilma-
hew in Dunbartonshire, by R. M. Kerr, 4to, Glasgow, 1847-9
(50).*

A History of the Napiers of Merchiston . . . , 4to, London, 1921.

Neale—Charters and Records of Neale of Berkeley Yate and Cor-
sham, by John Alexander Neale, 4to, Warrington, 1906-7*
(supplement, 1927, and addendum to supplement, 1929).

Need—A History of the Family of Need of Arnold, Nottinghamshire, by Michael L. Walker, 1963 (100).

Nelson—A Genealogical History of the Nelson Family, by Thomas James Nelson, 4to, Kings Lynn, 1908.

The Nelsons of Burnham Thorpe . . . , by M. Eyre Matcham, John Lane, 1911.

Nevill—History and Genealogical Account of the Noble Family of Nevill . . . , by D. Rowland, fo., London, 1830 (60, most of which the author destroyed).

History of the Family of Neville . . . , by H. Drummond, atlas fo., 1842 (from Drummond's Hist. of Noble Families, VIII).

A Sketch of the Stock of Nevill, Earls of Northumberland in the Saxon Times, and of its Descendants, Earls of Westmorland, by W. E. Surtees, Newcastle, 1843.

De Nova Villa, or the House of Nevill in Sunshine and Shade, by the Rev. H. J. Swallow, Newcastle, 1885.

The Nevills of Warwick, by F. E. Melton, Nelson, 1913.

New—Notes of English Families of the Name of New, by P. P. New, Rochdale, 4to, 1886.

Newbolt—Pedigree of the old Winton Family of the Newbolts, and Their Descendants, by E. D. Newbolt, Eastbourne, 1895.*

Newdigate—Origin and Early History . . . , by J. G. Nicholls, 1872 (not known to me as a separate work).

The Cheverels of Cheverel Manor, by Lady Newdigate-Newdegate, London, 1898.

Newmarch—The Newmarch Pedigree, verified by Public Records . . . , by G. F. and C. H. Newmarch, Cirencester, 1868.

Newport—Genealogical Account of the Family of Newport of High Ercall in the co. of Salop, afterwards Earls of Bradford, by G. T. O. Bridgeman, Bridgenorth, 4to, 37pp., n.d.

Newsom—Memorials of the Families of Newsom and Brigg, ed. by the Rev. J. E. Brigg, Huddersfield, 1898.*

Newton—Some Notices of the Family of Newton . . . , by T. H. Noyes junr., London, 1857.
Genealogical Memoranda relating to the Family of Newton, 12pp., 4to, London, 1871.

Nicholas—Genealogical Memoranda relating to the Family of Nicholas, by Major Griffin Nicholas, 4to, Hounslow, 1874.*

Nichols—The Hall of Lawford Hall, by F. M. Nichols, 1891.

Nicholson—Nicholson of Badworth . . . , originally of Carlton near Barnsley. . . , by T. N. Ince of Wakefield, 4to, 4pp., 1861.
Clan Nicholson, by J. G. Nicholson, Edin., 1938.
Memorials of the Family of Nicholson of Blackshaw..., collected by Francis Nicholson, ed. by E. Axon, Kendal, 1928.*

Nicol—The Genealogy of the Nicol Family (Kincardineshire), by W. E. Nicol, London, 1909.

Nicolls—History of the Nicolls Family, with a Genealogical Tree, by William Jasper Nicolls, n.d., 99pp., (100).*

Nisbet, Nesbitt—History of the Family of Nisbet or Nesbitt in Scotland and Ireland, by Alexander Nesbitt . . . completed by his Widow Cecilia Nesbitt, 4to, Torquay, 1898.*
Nisbet of that Ilk, by R. C. Nesbitt, London, John Murray, 4to, 1841.
History of the Nesbitt Family, by R. Nesbitt, 1930.

Nixon—See French.

Noble—An Account of the Families of Noble of Ardmore and Noble of Ardkinglas, by Sir Andrew Noble, 2nd edn., fo., 1971.*

Noel—Some Letters and Records of the Noel Family, comp. by

Emilia F. Noel, St Catherine Press, 1910.

Norris—A Memoir of the Lancashire House of Noreis or Norres, by G. Ormerod, Liverpool, 1850.

North—Lives of the Norths . . . , by the Hon. Roger North, 3v., London, 1826.

Northcote—The Life of the late Earl of Iddesleigh . . . and a Complete History of the Northcote Family, by C. Worthy, London, 1887.

Norwood—The Norwoods, by G. M. Norwood, Bushey Heath, 1963-5 (500).

Nott—Nott Family Memorials, 4to, 1879.*

O

Oakley—The Oakley Pedigree, by E. F. Oakley, Mitchell Hughes and Clarke, 1934 (50). (?pedigree only)

O'Brien—Historical Memoirs of the O'Briens . . . , by John O'Donoghue, Dublin, 1860.
The O'Briens, by W. A. Lindsay, London and Aylesbury, 1876.
Genealogical Notes of the O'Briens of Kilcor, co. Cork, 1887.*
History of the O'Briens . . . , by the Hon. Donough O'Brien Batsford, 4to, 1949.

O'Connor—Memoir of Charles O'Conor of Balanagare, with a Historical Account of the Family of O'Conor, by the Rev. C. O'Conor, Dublin, 1796.
Memoir of the O'Connors of Balintabber, co. Roscommon, by R. O'Conor, Dublin, 1857.
The O'Connors of Connaught, comp. from the MS. of John O'Donovan, with addns. by the Rt. Hon. C. O. O'Connor

Don, 4to, Dublin, 1891.*

O'Davoren—The O'Davorens of Cathermacnaughten, by G. U. Mac-namara, Limerick, 1912-13.

O'Dempsey—An Account of the O'Dempseys, Chiefs of the Clan Maline, by Thomas Mathews, Dublin, 1903.

O'Dwyer—The O'Dwyers of Kilmanagh, by Sir Michael O'Dwyer, Murray, 1933.

Ogilvie, Ogilvy—In Defence of the Regalia 1651-52; being Select-ions from the Family Papers of the Ogilvies of Barras, by the Rev. Douglas Gordon Barron, London, 1910.
The House of Airlie, by the Rev. William Wilson, 2v., Murray, 1924.
The Ogilvies of Boyne, by Alastair and Henrietta Tayler, Aber-deen U. P., 1933.
The Ogilvies of Termenny, by A. S. Ogilvie, Edin., 1938.
The Ogilvies of Banff, by C. D. Abercromby, 1939.

Oglander—Oglander Memoirs . . . , ed. by W. H. Long, 4to, New-port, I.O.W., 1888.

Ogle—An Account of the Family of Ogle, 8vo, Edin., 1812.*
Ogle and Bothal . . . , by Sir Henry A. Ogle, Bt., 4to, New-castle, 1902.

Ogstoun—Genealogical History of the Family of Ogstoun, by Alexander Ogstoun, Edin., 1871 and 1876 (supplement 1897).

O'Hart—The Last Princess of Tara, or a Brief Sketch of the O'Hart Ancient Royal Family, by John O'Hart, Dublin, 1873.

O'Laverty—Some Account of the Surname of O'Laverty, O'Lafferty, Laverty or Lafferty, by the Rev. James O'Laverty, 8vo, 24pp., wrapper, 1891.

Oldfield—A History of the Oldfield Family, by H. Oldfield, 1936.

Oliphant—The Jacobite Lairds of Gask, by T. L. Oliphant, Grampian Club, 1870.

The Oliphants in Scotland . . . , ed. by Joseph Anderson, 4to, Edin., 1879 (100).*

The Oliphants of Gask . . . , by E. Maxtone Graham (E. Blair Oliphant), Nisbet, 1910.

Oliver—The Olivers of Cloghanodfoy, by Maj.-Gen. J. R. Oliver, ? 1894; 2nd edn., London, 1897; 3rd edn., A. and N. C. S. Ltd., 1904.

O'Madden—Genealogical Historical and Family Records of the O'Maddens of Hy-Many . . . , by T. H. Madden, Dublin, 1894.

O'Meagher—Some Historical Notices of the O'Meaghers of Ikerrin, by J. C. O'Meagher, 4to, London, 1886 (re-published New York, 1890).

O'Neill—The O'Neills of Ulster, their History and Genealogy, by Thomas Mathews, 3v., Dublin, 1907.

Onslow—The Onslow Family, by C. E. Vulliamy, Chapman and Hall, 1953.

O'Reilly—A Genealogical History of the O'Reillys . . . , 18th Century, ed. by James Carney, Cavan, 1959.

Orlebar—The Orlebar Chronicles . . . (The Children of the Manor House), by F. St John Orlebar, vol. 1, all published, 4to, Mitchell Hughes and Clarke, 1930 (250).

Ormerod—Parentalia . . . , by George Ormerod, 1851; additions and index, 1856.*

Ormesby—Pedigree of the Family of Ormesby formerly of Ormsby in Lincolnshire, now in Ireland, ed. by J. F. Fuller, 4to, London, 1887.

Ormiston—The Ormistons of that Ilk, by T. L. Ormiston, 8pp., 1905; 2nd edn. by W. J. Ormiston, 1933.
The Ormistons of Teviotdale, by T. L. Ormiston, 4to, Exeter, 1951.

O'Rourke—Origin of the O'Rourkes with a History of the Sept., comp. by Anthony Mathews, Dublin, 1970.

Orpen—The Orpen Family . . . , by G. H. Orpen, Butler and Tanner, 1930.*

Osborne—Osborne Genealogy, with Notes, by J. J. Howard, 4to, 1864.*

Osler—Lions in the Way, by Anne Wilkinson, Macmillan, 1957.

O'Toole—Les O'Toole; Notice sur le clan ou la tribu des O'Toole . . . dans la province de Leinster . . . , ed. by C. D. O'Kelly Farrell, fo., La Réole, 1864.
History of the Clan O'Toole and other Leinster Septs, by the Rev. P. L. O'Toole, O.C.C., 4to, Dublin, 1890.
The O'Tooles, anciently lords of Powerscourt, Ferture, and Tinale . . . , by John O'Toole, Dublin, n.d.

Otter—Pedigree of the Family of Otter of Welham, by Capt. A. E. Lawson Lowe, 4to, London, 1880.*

Ottley—Records of an Ancient Family, by J. E. Ottley, 1923.

Ouseley–Genealogy of the Ouseley Family, comp. by Richard Kelly
revised by his surviving relations, Dunmor, ? 1899.

Owen–Memories of the Ancient Family of Owen of Orielton, by
J. R. Phillips, Chiswick Press, 1886 (25 copies on hand made
paper).

Oxley-Parker–The Oxley-Parker Family in Suffolk and Essex, by
O. D. Parker, 1925.

P

Palmer–Pedigree of the Ancient Family of the Palmers of Sussex,
1672, with Additions by Roger Jenyns, 4to, London, 1867.
A Genealogical and Historical Account of the Family of Palmer of Kenmare . . . , comp. by the Rev. A. H. H. Palmer,
paper, London, 1872.
Pedigree of the Palmer Family of South Molton and Torrington, Devon, revised by F. T. Colby, 4to, Exeter, 1892 (50).
The Early History of the Palmer Family, by G. H. Palmer, 1918.
A Pineapple for the King, by T. W. E. Roche, Phillimore, 1971.

Parker–Genealogical Memoranda relating to the Family of Parker
of Upton House . . . , by E. M. S. Parker, fo., Bristol, 1899.
See also Oxley-Parker.

Parshall–The Parshall Family, A.D. 870-1913, by H. F. Parshall,
4to, Glasgow, 1915 (100);* suppt., 1931.

Parkinson–The Parkinson Family of Lancashire, by Richard
Ainsworth, 4to, 1932-6.*

Partridge–Pedigree . . . Notes . . . Partridge Family . . . of Gloucestershire, by C. Harold Partridge, Edgbaston, 1903.

Paston–The Paston Letters, 2v., 1787; ed. by James Gairdner,

12mo, 3v., Birmingham, 1872-5 (and others).
Account of the Paston Family, by F. Worship, 1852 (25).*

Paton—Records of the Paton Family, ed. by J. H. Paton, 12pp., Edin., 1889.*

Pattinson—The Pattinsons of Kirklington, by J. F. Chance, 1899.*

Paul—Some Pauls of Glasgow and their Descendants, by Sir James Balfour Paul, Edin., 1912 (35).*

Paycocke—The Paycockes of Coggleshall, by E. Power, 1920.

Pearson—The History of the Pearson Family, by Angus Baxter, 1949.

Pease—The Pease Family of Essex, York and Durham, by J. H. Bell, fo., 1872.
Pease of Darlington . . . , by Joseph Foster, 4to, 1891.*

Peche—Peche of Lullingstone, by the Rev. W. A. Scott Robertson, London, 1886.

Peck—The Book of Pecks, by H. W. Peck, Liverpool, 1964.

Peel—The Peels; a Family Sketch, by Jonathan Peel, London, 1877.*

Peers—Genealogical History of the Peers Family (of Alveston, co. Warwick), by M. R. W. Peers Adams, fo., wrappers, Simla, 1892 (also 'A Selection . . . ' imp. 8vo).
See also Adams.

Peile—Annals of the Peiles of Strathclyde . . . , by the Rev. T. W. Peile, 1899.

Pelham—Historical and Genealogical Notices of the Pelham Family,

by Mark Anthony Lower, 4to, and fo., 1873.*
Some Early Pelhams, by the Hon. Mrs Arthur Pelham and
David MacLean, Hove, 1931.

Pelly—The Pelly Family in England, by D. R. Pelly, 1918.*

Pemberton—Pemberton Pedigrees, comp. by Maj.-Gen. R. C. B.
Pemberton, ed. by the Rev. R. Pemberton, Bedford, 1923.

Penn—A Pedigree and Genealogical Notes . . . , of the Family of
Penn of England and America, by James Coleman, 4to, and
8vo, London, 1871.
Further Light on the Ancestry of William Penn, by Brig. O. F. G.
Hogg, paper, Soc. Gen., 1964.
See also Pennington.

Penney—My Ancestors . . . , by Norman Penney, 4to, London,
1920 (250).*

Pennington—The Penns and Penningtons of the Seventeenth
Century, by Maria Webb, Dublin, 1867 and Philadelphia,
1868.
See also Askew and Penn.

Pennyman—Records of the Family of Pennyman of Ormesby,
comp. by James Worsley Pennyman, York, 1904.*

Peploe—See Browne.

Pepys—Genealogy of the Pepys Family 1273-1887, by W. C. Pepys,
4to, London, 1887, 1951, 1971; supplement by Lord Cott-
enham, 1963.
Eight Generations of the Pepys Family, 1500-1800, by Edwin
Chappell, Blackheath, 1936 (500).*

Perceval, Percival—A Brief Account of the Family of Perceval,

Earls of Egmont, 32pp., 12mo., London, 1740.

The Percival Book, by Dr A. C. Percival and Brig. E. L. Percival, D.S.O., London, 1970 (150).*

See also Yvery.

Percy—Extract of the History and Genealogy of the Noble Families of the Earl and Countess of Northumberland, by Richard Griffith, 8vo, 60pp., Dublin, 1764.*

Annals of the House of Percy . . . , by E. B. de Fonblanque, 2v., London, 1887.*

A History of the House of Percy . . . , by G. Brenan, ed. by W. A. Lindsay, 4to, 2v., London, 1902 (150 on large paper).

Perigal—Some Account of the Perigal Family, comp. by F. Perigal, 8vo, 1887.*

Perkins—The History of Ufton Court . . . in the co. of Berks and of the Perkins Family, by A. M. Sharp, 4to, London, 1892.

Perton—Connected Annals of the Manor and Family of Perton of Perton, co. Staffs . . . , by E. A. Hardwicke, 4to, Calcutta, 1897.

Phillimore—Genealogy of the Family of Phillimore, by W. P. W. Phillimore, Pt. 1. 1903; Pt. 2 by Lord Phillimore, Devizes, 1922.

See also Fynmore.

Petty-Fitzmaurice—Glenrought and the Petty Fitzmaurice, by the Earl of Lansdowne, O.U.P., 1937.

Philip—The Story of the House of Philip, by G. Philip, 1934.

Phillips—The Phillips Family of Brighton, by D. Hannon, 1938.*

Phipps—Notes on the Phipps and Phip Families, by Maj. H. R. Phipps, (in parts) 4to, Lahore, 1911.

Picard—The Picards or Pychards of Stradewy (now Tretowen) Castle, and Scethrog . . . with some Account of the Family of Sapy of Upper Sapey . . . , roy. 8vo, London, 1878.

Pickering—The Pickerings of Barlby and Wetherby, by P. S. Umfreville, 1916.

Pilkington—Genealogy of the Pilkingtons of Lancashire, comp. by John Harland, ed. by W. E. A. Axon, 4to, 1875 (109);* and 1886.
    History of the Lancashire Family of Pilkington . . . , by Lt. Col. J. Pilkington, 4to, Liverpool, 1894 (180); 2nd edn., Liverpool, 1912.*
    Harland's Pilkingtons, by R. G. Pilkington, 4th edn., Dublin, 1906.

Pitcairn—The History of the Fife Pitcairns, by Constance Pitcairn, Blackwood, 1905.

Pitman—History and Pedigree of the Family of Pitman of Dunchideock, by Charles E. Pitman, London, 1920 (125).
    Frederick Cobbe Pitman and his Family, by H. A. Pitman, Adlard, 1930.*

Pitt—The House of Pitt, by Sir Tresham Lever, Murray, 1947.

Plaisted—The Plaisted Family of North Wilts., by Arthur H. Plaisted, Westminster Pub. Co., 1939.

Playfair—Notes on the Scottish Family of Playfair, by the Rev.
A. G. Playfair, 1906; 3rd edn., Tunbridge Wells, 1913;
Supplement to the above, 1919; 4th edn., Tunbridge
Wells (as The Playfair Book), 1932.

Playford—History of the Playford Family of Suffolk, by Lord
Arthur Hervey, Lowestoft, 1858.

Pledge—The History of the Pledge Family; with the Barrow
Ancestry, ed. by G. C. Keech, 1970.

Plowden—Records of the Plowden Family, by B. M. Plowden,
4to., 1887.*
Records of the Chicheley Plowdens . . . , by W. F. C. Chicheley
Plowden, 4to, London, 1914.

Plumpton—Historical and Biographical Notice of the Family of
Plumpton of Plumpton, co. York, 4to, Camden Soc.,
1839.

Poe—The Origin and Early History of the Family of Poë or Poe,
by Sir E. T. Bewley, Dublin, 1906 (200).*

Pollock—The Family of Pollock of Newry . . . , by the Rev. A. S.
Hartigan, Folkstone, 1901.

Pomeroy—The House of de la Pomerai, by E. B. Powley, 4to,
Liverpool U.P., 1944 (250).

Ponsonby—The Ponsonby Family, by Maj.-Gen. Sir John Ponsonby, K.C.B., Medici Soc., 1929; reprinted 1970.

Poole—The Pooles of Cae Nest, Merionethshire, by H. R. Poole,
ed. by A. G. Hunter, 4to, Horncastle, 1916.*
The Pooles of Mayfield, by R. ffolliott, Dublin, 1958.

Pope—Pope, his Descendants and Family Connections, by Joseph Hunter, London, 1857.

Portal—The Portal Family, 4to, London, 1863.
The Portals of Laverstoke, by Sir W. Portal, 1921.

Porterfield—See Boyd.

Poulett—The Pouletts of Hinton St George, by Colin G. Winn, 4to, 1975.

Powell—Pedigree of the Family of Powell and Baden-Powell . . ., ed. by Edgar Powell, 4to, Clowes, 1926.

Poyntz—An Historical and Genealogical Memoir of the Family of Poyntz, by Sir John Maclean, 2v., 4to, Exeter, 1886 (75).*

Pratt—The Family of Pratt of Gawsworth, Carrigrohane, co. Cork, by John Pratt, D.S.C., Millom, 1925; one 2nd edn., as Pratt Family Records, Millom, 1931.
Lord Chancellor Camden and His Family, by H. S. Eeles, Philip Allan, 1934.

Prichard—Genealogy of the Descendants of the Prichards . . . , by the Rev. T. G. Smart, Enfield, 1868.*
Memorials of the Prichards of Almeley, by Isabel Southall, 4to, Birmingham, 1893; 2nd edn., 1901.

Prickett—The Pricketts of Allerthorpe, by F. F. Prickett, 1918;* 2nd edn., 4to, Mitchell Hughes and Clarke, 1929.*

Prideaux—Memoir of the Families of Prideaux and Brune, 1874.

Primrose—History of the Primrose-Roseberry Family 1500-1900, by J. Macbeth Forbes, London, 1907.

Pringle—The Records of the Pringles of Hoppringills of the Scottish border, by Alexander Pringle, Edin., 1933.

Probyn—See Hopkins.

Prowse—Notes on the Family of Prowse of Compton Bishop, co. Somerset, by E. F. Wade, London, 4to, 1879.*

Pulleyn—The Pulleyns of Yorkshire, by Catherine Pullein, 4to, Leeds, 1915.

Punchard—Punchard of Heanton Punchardon . . . , by E. G. Punchard, D.D., 3pts in 4, 4to, 1894.

Pyke—See Halley.

Q

Quinchant—See Kinchant.

Quatremain—The Quartremains of Oxfordshire, by W. F. Carter, O.U.P., 1936.

R

Radcliffe, Radclyffe—Genealogy of the Family of Radclyffe of Dilston, Northumberland, by James Ellis, 4to, Newcastle, 1850.
  Radclyffe Tracts: the Heirs General to Radclyffe of Derwentwater, 4to, Newcastle, 1859 (100).
  The Radcliffes of Leigh, by E. M. Darlington, 4to, Stockport, 1918.*
  The Book of the Radclyffes, by Charles P. Hampson, 4to, 1940.*

Raikes—Historical and Biographical Account of the Raikes Family, London and Northampton, 8vo, 1881; an edn., with continuations and additions by C. F. Raikes, fo., 1930 (100).*

Rainsford–The Rainsford Family, by Emily A. Buckland, Worcester, Caxton Press, 1933.

Raleigh–Raleigh Genealogy; with the Life of Sir Walter Raleigh . . . , by Edward Edwards, 2v., 1868.

Ram–The Ram Family, by W. and F. R. Ram, 1940.

Rankin–The Rankins, pipers to the Macleods of Duart, by Henry Whyte, Glasgow, 1907.

Ransford–The Origins of the Ransfords . . . , by Alfred Ransford, London, 1919.

Rathbone–Records of the Rathbone Family of Liverpool, by E. A. Rathbone, 1913.*

Ravenscroft–Some Ravenscrofts, by W. Ravenscroft, Milford-on-Sea, 1929.

Ravenshaw–History of the Ravenshaw Family, particularly of Cheshire, by W. C. Renshaw, Q.C., London, 1900 (30).*
History of Ravenshaw of Ash, Richmond and Badington, by John Ravenshaw, London, London, 1906 (90).*

Rawdon–The Rawdon Papers . . . , ed. by the Rev. Edward Berwick, London, 1819.
The Life of Marmaduke Rawdon of York . . . with Chart and Pedigree of the Family, 4to, Camden Soc., 1863.

Rawle–Records of the Family of Rawle of Somerset, by E. J. Rawle, Taunton, 1898 (75).*

Raymond–Genealogical Memoranda relating to the Family of Raymond of Kintbury, Berks, by R. S. Boddington, 4to,

1886.*

Reade, Rede, Reed, Reid—A Record of the Redes of Barton Court
. . . (with an Account of the Reades of Rossenara, by R. R.
Macmullen), by the Rev. Compton Reade, 4to, and 8vo,
Hereford, 1899.
The Reades of Blackwood Hill in the Parish of Horton,
Staffs . . . , by A. L. Reade, 4to, London, 1906 (350).*
The Barons Reid-Robertson of Straloch, by the Rev. James
Robertson, 4to, Blairgowrie, 1887.
A Register of Reeds . . . , comp. by L. Reed, 4to, 1937.*
The Reids of Kittochside, by Herbert Reid, Pt. 1., Glasgow,
1943; Pt. 2., Glasgow, 1945.

Redman—The Redmans of Levens and Harewood, by W. Green-
wood, Kendal, 1903; 2nd edn., 4to, Highgate, 1905.
The Redmans of Halfway House, by C. B. O'Grady (in progress).

Rennie—The Rennies of Kilsyth, by J. E. Rennie, Constable,
1965-7.

Renton—The Family of Renton, thin post 8vo, c. 1881 (some on
parchment paper, one side only).

Rentoul—A Record of the Family and Lineage of James Alexander Rentoul, comp. by Erminda Rentoul, Belfast, 1890.

Richardson—The Annals of the Cleveland Richardsons and their
Descendants, by George Richardson, 12mo., Newcastle-on-
Tyne, 1850.*
Records of a Quaker Family, the Richardsons of Cleveland, by
A. O. Boyce, 4to, London, 1889.
See also Horton.

Richmond—Richmond Family Records, by H. I. Richmond,
Adlard, Vol. 1., 1933, mostly families in U.S.A.;

Vol. 2., 1935, mostly with Wiltshire families, including Webb; Vol. 3., 1938, deals with the descendants of Rycheman of Binknoll, Broad Hinton, Wilts.

Richold—Records of the Richold Family, by F. H. and S. L. Richold, Tonbridge, 1954.

Rickards—Rickards of Evenjobb and his Descendants, by Robert Rickards, Cardiff, 1905.

Riddell—History of the Ancient Ryedales . . . , by G. T. Ridlon, Manchester, 1884.

Ridge—The Ridge Family of Sussex, by Dudley Ridge, Phillimore, 1974.

Riland—Three Hundred Years of a Family Living, being a History of the Rilands of Sutton Coldfield, by the Rev. W. K. Riland Bedford, 4to, Birmingham, 1889;* (also fifty on large paper).

Rivett-Carnac—Notes on the Family of Rivett-Carnac, by J. H. Rivett Carnac, 1909.*

Rivington—The Publishing House of Rivington, ed. by Septimus Rivington, 1894; 2nd edn., 1919.

Roberts—Some Memorials of the Family of Roberts of Queen's Tower, Sheffield, by S. Roberts, Sheffield, 1862, 1924, 1971.
A Roberts Family, Quondam Quakers of Queen's County, by E. J. A. Impey, 1939.

Robertson—The History and Martial Achievements of the Robertsons of Strowan . . . , by the Hon. Alexander Robertson of Strowan, 12mo., Edin., 1771-85.

Stemmata Robertson et Durdin (Robertsons of Groundwater), by Herbert Robertson, London, 1893-5.*

A Brief Account of the Clan Donnachaidh . . . , by David Robertson, sm. 4to, Glasgow, 1894.

Genealogy of the Family of Robertson of Newbigging, Orkney, by A. W. Johnston, 11pp., Coventry, 1909.*

The Chiefs of the Clan Donnachaidh . . . , by J. Robertson.

A Short History of the Clan Robertson, by J. Robertson Reid, Stirling, 1933.

The Family of Robert Robertson of Prenderguest and Brownbank . . . , comp. by S. Eustace, 28pp., pamph., Harrison and Sons, 1931.

The Robertsons: Clan Donnachaidh of Athol, by Sir Iain Moncreiffe, Bt., 1954.

See also Douglas, Forbes-Robertson and Reid.

Robbins, Robin, Robins—Gleanings of the Robin Family, by A. Robin, Mowbray, 1880.

Gleanings of the Robins or Robbins Family of England, by the Rev. Mills Robbins, 2nd edn., Devizes, 1908.*

Robinson—Some Account of the Family of Robinson of the White House, Appleby, by C. B. Norcliffe, Westminster, 1874.*

Genealogical Memoirs of the Family of Brooke Robinson of Dudley . . . , by Brooke Robinson, M.P., 4to, Nicholls and Sons, 1896 (30).*

The Robinson Family of Bolsover and Chesterfield, by P. M. Robinson and A. L. Spence, 1937; supplement, 1961.*

See also Shorthouse.

Roby—Pedigree of Roby of Castle Donington, co. Leicester, by Henry J. Roby, Manchester, 1888; 2nd edn., 1889; also 4to, 69pp., 1907.*

Roger, Rogers—The Scottish Branch of the Norman House of

Roger, with a Genealogical Account of the Family of Playfair, by the Rev. Charles Rogers, London, 1872 (100); 2nd
edn., Edin., 1875.*

Some Account of the Rogers in Cupar Grange, by J. C. Roger,
London, 1877.

An Historical Summary of the Roger Renants of Cupar, by
J. C. Roger, London, 1879 (125).*

History of our Family, Rogers of Westmeon, 1451-1902, by
J. C. Roger, 4to, London, 1902.*

The Family of Roger in Aberdeenshire, by Kenneth Rogers,
1920.

Rokeby–Oeconomia Rokebiorum, by Ralph Rokeby, ed. by
A. W. C. Hallen, Edin., 1887.

Rolfe–Rolfe Family Records, by R. T. and A. Gunther, 1914
(112).*

Rolland–Disblair 1634-1884 . . . , by A. Walker, 4pp., Aberdeen,
1884.

Roos–See Ingilby.

Roscoe–Roscoeana, being some Account of the Kinsfolk of
William Roscoe of Liverpool . . . , by F. W. Dunston, 1905
(132).*

Rose–A Genealogical Deduction of the Family of Rose of Kilravock, written 1683-4 by the Rev. Hew Rose, continued by
the Rev. Lachlan Shaw in 1753, ed. by Cosmo Innes for
the Spalding Club, 4to, 1848.

The Roses of Kilravock, by J. Skelton, 1883.

The Domestic Papers of the Rose Family, ed. by Alastair and
Henrietta Tayler, Aberdeen, 1926.

Genealogy of the Family of Rose of Holme Rose, by Henry Rose,
Nairn, 1929.

History of the Family of de Ros, de Rose, Rose of Kilravock,
  by E. H. Rose, Frome, 1939.

Ross—Ane Breve Chronicle of the Earlis of Ross . . . including Ross
  of Balnagown, ed. by W. R. Baillie, 4to, Edin., 1850.
  Rosses of Glencalvie, by John Robertson, 1844.
  A Genealogical Account of the Rosses of Dalton . . . , by George
  Parker Knowles, London, 8pp., 1855 (75).*
  History of the Clan Ross . . . , by Alexander M. Ross, Dingwall,
  North Star Office, 1932.
  The Clan Ross, by Donald MacKinnon, Edin., 1957.

Row—Memorial of the Family of Row, ed. by James Maidment,
  4to, Edin., 1828 (40).

Rowdon—Rowdon of Rowdon, co. York, by John Rodon or Rod-
  en, 4to, Dublin, 31pp., n.d.

Rowntree—The Rowntrees of Riseborough, by C. B. Rowntree,
  Saffron Walden, 1940.

Royden—Three Royden Families, written by John Brownbill for
  E. B. Royden, Edin., 4to, 1924.*

Royds—The Pedigree of the Family of Royds, by Sir C. M. Royds,
  C.B., 4to, London, 1910.

Rudd—Records of the Rudd Family, by M. A. Rudd, 4to, Bristol,
  1920.

Ruddiman—Notes on the Ruddimans in Scotland, by G. Harvey
  Johnston, 4to, Edin., 1887 (25).
  The Ruddimans in Scotland, their History and Works, by G.
  Harvey Johnston, 4to, Edin., 1901 (21).*

Russell—An Historical and Exact Account of the Origin and Rise of the Russells, Earls of Bedford . . . , by A. L., 12mo., London, 1684.

Historical Memoirs of . . . the House of Russell, by J. H. Wiffen, 2v., fo., and 3v., 8vo, London, 1833 (see Round, Peerage and Family History, ch. 6).

A Sketch of the History of the House of Russell, by David Ross, Liverpool and London, 18mo, 1848.

The Russells of Birmingham in the French Revolution and in America, 1791-1814, by S. H. Jeyes, ed. by D. Hannay, London, 1911.

Two Centuries of Family History . . . , by Gladys Scott Thomson, Longmans Green, 1930.

The Russells in Bloomsbury, by G. S. Thomson, 1940.

The Russells, by Christopher Trent, Muller, 1966.

Rutherford–The Rutherfords of that Ilk and their Cadets . . . , by T. H. Cockburn Hood, ed. by the Rev. W. MacLeod, 4to, Edin., 1884 (A supplementary volume with corrections etc., by C. H. E. Carmichael was printed in 1889-03 but not circulated. There is a copy in the L.O.)

Ruthven–The Ruthven of Freeland Peerage . . . , by J. H. Stevenson, 4to, Glasgow, 1905.

Rutter–The Family of Le Roter or Rutter, comp. by W. H. Wingate, 1966.*

Rye–An Account of the Family of Rye, by Walter Rye, London, 1876.*

S

Sackville–Memoirs of the Ancient and Noble Family of Sackville, by Arthur Collins, London, 1741.

An Historical and Topographical Sketch of Knole . . . and the Sackville Family, by J. Bridgeman, London, 1797; several other editions including 1817, 1821, and 1827.

Knole and the Sackvilles, by V. Sackville-West, 1922; other
editions 1947/8 and 1958.

History of the Sackville Family, together with a Description of
Knole . . . , ed. by Charles J. Phillips, 2v., 4to, 1929.

Sackville of Drayton, by L. Marlow, 1948.

Saintclair, St Clair, Sinclair—Genealogy of the Sinclairs of Ulb-
ster, by Sir John Sinclair, Bt., 1910.

Genealogie of the Saintclaires of Rosslyn, by Father R. A.
Hay, ed. by James Maidment, 4to, Edin., 1835 (108 on
small paper, 12 on large).

The Sinclairs of England, by Thomas Sinclair, London, 1887.

The Saint-Clairs of the Isles . . . , ed. by R. W. Saint-Clair, 4to,
Auckland, 1898.

Histoire Généalogique de la Famille de Saint-Clair . . . , by
L. A. Saint-Clair, Paris, 1905.

The Sinclairs of Brabsterdorran, Caithness, by Roland St Clair,
4v., Coventry, 1911.

Sainthill—The Sainthill Family, by A. St Hill, 1938.

St John—Notitia St Johannia, Genealogical Memoir of the Family
of St John, 8vo, 1713.

Salmond—Memoir as to the Surname of Salmond, by George Salmond, Glasgow, n.d.

Salmond of Waterfoot, by A. L. Salmond, 4to, 1887 (25).*

Sandeman—Sandeman Genealogy, by Lt. Col. J. Glas Sandeman,
4to, Edin., 1895; 2nd edn., by G. L. Sandeman, Edin., 1950.

The Sandeman Family of Perth, by W. A. Sandeman, 1926.

Sandilands—Sandilands of Crabstone, 4to, 1863.*

Sandwith—The Sandwiths of Helmsley, co. York, by L. S., 1897.

The Sandwiths of the City of York, by L. Sandwith, 1921.

Sandys–Some Notes for a History for the Sandys Family of Great
Britain, Ireland, etc., by Vivian Comely, ed. by Col. T. M.
Sandys, M.P., 4to, London, 1907.*
History of the Family of Sandys of Cumberland . . . , by E. S.
Sandys, Barrow Printing Co., 1930.*

Sankey–Memorials of the Family of Sankey A.D. 1207-1880,
(printed from the Genealogical Collections of C. S. Best-
Gardner), Swansea, 1880.*

Sapy–See Picard.

Saunders–The Saunders Family History, comp. by Major R. T.
Saunders, R.A., assisted by J. A. Macklin, sm. 4to, 1928.

Saunderson–The Saundersons of Castle Saunderson, by Henry
Saunderson, 1936.*

Savage–A Genealogical History of the Savage Family in Ulster,
by G. F. Savage Armstrong, 1906.

Scaife–The Scaife Family of Cumberland and Westmorland, by
M. M. Scaife, Exeter, Pollard, 1925.

Scattergood–The Scattergoods and the East India Company,
1619-1723, ed. by Sir R. C. Temple, Bt., L. M. Anstey, and
B. P. Scattergood, Bombay, British India Press, 1921; also
4to, Harpenden, D. J. Jefferey, 1935 (25).

Sclater–Records of the Family of Sclater, by C. E. L. Sclater,
Newport, 1967.

Scott–A True History of Several Honourable Families of the
Right Honourable Name of Scot, by Capt. Walter Scot of
Satchell, 4to, Edin., 1688; reprinted Hawick, 1786; another
edn., ed. by J. G. Winning, 4to, Hawick, 1894 (240).*

Metrical History . . . Scot and Elliott . . . , by Capt. Walter
Scot of Satchell, 4to, Edin., 1688; reprinted 1776 and 4to,
Edin., 1892 (50).*

Pedigree of Scott of Stokoe, comp. by William Scott, M.D.,
Newcastle, 1783 and Edin., 1827; with continuation by
John Gray Bell, London, 1852 (75), and 1882.*

Memorials of the Family of Scott of Scots Hall, co. Kent, by
James R. Scott, 4to, London, 1876.*

Genealogical Memoirs of the Family of Sir Walter Scott, Bt., by
Charles Rogers, Grampian Club and R. Hist. Soc., 1877.

The Scotts of Buccleuch, by Sir William Fraser, 4to, 2v., Edin.,
1878 (150).

The Scots of Ewesdale, by T. J. Carlyle, Hawick, 1884.

Upper Teviotdale and the Scotts of Buccleuch . . . , by J. R.
Scott-Oliver, 4to, Hawick, 1887 (also 50 copies on What-
man handmade paper).

A Short Genealogical and Historical Account of the Family of
Scott of Buccleuch, by Andrew Crichton, Dumfries, 1827.

The Scotts of Harperig, by J. A. Inglis, 4to, 1914.

Scott 1118-1923, being a Collection of Scott Pedigrees, by
Keith S. M. Scott, London, 1923 (170); 2nd edn., 1924.

Lesudden House and the Scots of Raeburn, by Sir Tresham
Lever, Boydell Press, 1971.

See also Napier.

Scroggs—The Family of Scroggs, by J. R. Dunlop, 4to, 1929.*

Scull—The Family of Scull, by William Le Hardy.

Seaton, Seton, Setoun, Seytoun—History of the House of Seytoun
to the year 1559, by Sir Richard Maitland of Lethington,
continued to 1687 by Alexander Viscount Kingston, ed. by
J. Fullarton, for the Bannatyne and Maitland Clubs, 4to, Glasgow, 1829 (71);* also 101 copies printed off on Bannatyne
Club paper.

The Genealogy of the House and Surname of Setoun, by Sir

Richard Maitland; with the Chronicle of the House of Set-oun, compiled in metre by James Kamington, alias Peter Manye, ed. by C. K. Sharpe, 4to, Edin., 1830.

A History of the Family of Seton during Eight Centuries, by George Seton, 4to, 2v., Edin., 1896-7 (212).*

The Last of the Setons of Parbroath, and their Cadets, by Col. Robert Seton Marshall, Edin., 1925.

Segrave—The Segrave Family, 1066-1935 . . . , by Charles W. Segrave, 1936-7 (200).

Selby—Selbyana; an Attempt to Elucidate the History of Selby of Wavendon, 8vo, Carlisle, 1825.

Sempill—The Poems of the Sempills of Beltrees . . . with Notes and Biographical Notices . . . , by James Peterson, 1849.

Serjeantson—Genealogical History of the Serjeantson of Hanlith, by the Rev. R. M. Serjeantson, 4to, Northampton, 1908.

Sewell—The Sewells of the Isle of Wight, by M. C. Owen, Manchester, 1906.*

Seymour—Wulfhall and the Seymours, by J. E. Jackson, 4to, 1874.
Annals of the Seymour Family from Early Times, by H. St Maur, London, 1902 (250); another edn., 1905.
The history and Romance of the Seymour Family, by A. A. Locke, Constable, 1911.
See also Somerset.

Shakespeare—Prolusions Genealogical and Biographical on the Family of Shakespeare . . . , by the Rev. Joseph Hunter, 1844.
Original Memoirs and Historical Accounts . . . Shakespeare . . . and Hart . . . , by John Jordan, ed. by J. O. Halliwell, 4to, London, 1865 (10).
Shakespeariana Genealogica . . . , by George R. French, London, 1869.

Shakespeares Family . . . , by Mrs C. C. Stopes, London, 1901.

John Shakespeare (1619-1689) of Shadwell and his Descendants, by Col. J. Shakespeare, Northumberland Press, 1931 (140).*

Shallross, Shawcross—A Brief Lineage; Shallross or Shawcross Pedigrees, by the Rev. W. H. Shawcross, Evesham, 1896.

Shallcross Pedigrees . . . , by the Rev. W. H. Shawcross, assisted by W. Gilbert, Index by Miss M. Wilson, fo., Hemsworth, 1908 (200).*

Shand—Some Notices of the Surname of Shand, by the Rev. George Shand, Norwich, 1877.*

Sharp, Sharpe—Life and Correspondence of Abraham Sharp . . . , with Memorials of his Family, by W. Cadworth, 4to, London, 1889.

The Sharpe Family, by T. E. Sharpe, 4to, 1901.

Shaw—Memorials of the Clan Shaw, by the Rev. W. G. Shaw, Dundee, 1868, Forfar, 1871 and 1881.*

A Genealogical Account of the Highland Families of Shaw, by Alexander M. Shaw, London, 1877 (100).*

Notes relating to some Shaws of Cheshire . . . , by W. C. Renshaw, fo., 1891 (30).*

The Records of a Lancastrian Family, by R. Cunliffe Shaw, 4to, Preston, 1940.*

History of the Clan Shaw, by Norman Shaw, Oxford, 1951.

Shaw of Shawbrook, of Ardandra Castle and of Antley (co. Longford), by J. C. M. Shaw, 1933.

Shawcross—See Shallross.

Sheldon—The Sheldons . . . of Worcestershire and Warwickshire, by E. A. B. Barnard, C.U.P., 1936.

Shelley—Memorials of the Family of Shelley of Great Yarmouth, by John Shelley of Plymouth, 4to, London, 1909 (100).*

Sheppard—Pedigree of the Family of Sheppard, by R. S. Boddington, 4to, London, 1883.
Brief History of the Sheppard Family, by W. A. Sheppard, Calcutta, 1891.

Sherborn—A History of the Family of Sherborn, by C. D. Sherborn, London, 1901 (250).

Sheridan—The Lives of the Sheridans, by Percy Fitzgerald, 2v., London, 1886.

Sherrington—History of Wigan Grammar School . . . with an Account of the Sherrington Family . . . , 2nd edn., by the Rev. G. C. Chambers, Wigan, 1937.

Shirley—Stemmata Shirleiana . . . , by E. P. Shirley, 4to, London, 1841 (100); 2nd edn., 4to, Westminster, 1873 (250).*

Shorthouse—Memorials of the Families of Shorthouse and Robinson . . . , by W. Ransom, Margaret Evans, and Isabel Southall, 4to, Birmingham, 1902.*

Shuttleworth—The House and Farm Accounts of the Shuttleworths of Gawthorpe Hall, Lancashire . . . , by John Harland, 4to, 4v., Chetham Society, 1856-58.

Sibthorp—Account of the Sibthorp Family, by A. R. Maddison, Lincoln, 1896.

Sidney, Sydney—An Account of the Sydney Family, Lee Priory Press, 1816 (from Collins Peerage).
Memoirs of the Sidney Family, by P. Sidney, 1899; another, entitled The Sidneys of Penshurst, 1901.

Siderfin—History of the Siderfin Family of West Somerset, by J. Sanders, Exeter, 1912.

Simpson—Simpson: Records of an Ancient Yeoman Family of the West Riding . . . 1544-1922, by Bt. Col. Stephen Simpson, Bemrose and Sons, 1922 (200).

Sinclair—See Saintclair.

Sing—The Family of Synge or Sing, by K. C. Synge, 1937.

Sitwell—The Sitwell Pedigree . . . , by Sir G. R. Sitwell, Bt., 4to, Scarborough, 1890 (20).*
A Brief History of Weston Hall, Northamptonshire, by Sir George Sitwell, Bt., London, 1927 (50).*
The Story of the Sitwells, by Sir G. R. Sitwell, Bt., 1946.

Sinton—Family and Genealogical Sketches, by the Rev. Thomas Sinton, Inverness, 1911.

Skene—Memorials of the Family of Skene of Skene, ed. by Williams Forbes Skene, D.C.L., 4to, Aberdeen, New Spalding Club, 1887 (525); sometimes one v. text and one v. pedigrees.

Skinner—A Notable Family of Scots Printers, by R. T. Skinner, Edin., 1927.
See also Chaplin.

Skipwith—A Brief Account of the Skipwiths of Newbold, Metheringham, and Prestwould, by F. Skipwith, Tunbridge Wells, 1867.*

Skottowe—The Leaf and the Tree, by P. F. Skottowe, 1963.

Skrine—Skrine of Warleigh . . . , by E. W. Ainley-Walker, 4to,

Wessex Press, 1936 (200).*

Slacke—Records of the Slacke Family in Ireland, by Helen A. Crofton, 4to, 19–.

Slyfield—Slyfield Manor and Family of Great Bookham, by J. H. Harvey and G. N. Slyfield, Horsham, 1953.

Smith, Smyth, Smythe—Notices relating to Thomas Smith of Campden, and to Henry Smith, sometime alderman of London, ? by C. P. Smith, 1836.

History of the Family of Smith of Nottingham, by Augustus Smith, M.P., fo., London, 1861.

Notice of the Family of Smith . . . formerly Lindsay, by the Rev. P. C. Campbell, 1869 (12).

Lives of the Lords of Strangford . . . , by E. B. de Fonblanque, London, 1877.

Annals of Smith of Cantley, Balby, and Doncaster, Yorks, by H. E. Smith, 4to, Sunderland, 1878.*

Some Account of the Smiths of Exeter and their Descendants, by A. M. Smith, Exeter, 1896.*

Some Account of the Family of Smith . . . of Shute, co. Devon, by W. P. W. Phillimore, 4to, London, 1900.*

The Smith Family; being a Popular Account of Most Branches of the Name . . . , by the Rev. Compton Reade, London, 1902; 'popular edition,' 1904, reprinted 1970.

The Gordons and Smiths at Minmore . . . (Smith of Glenlivet), by J. M. Bulloch, Huntly, 1910.

Notes and Illustrations concerning the Family History of James Smith of Coventry, comp. by Lady Durning Lawrence, London, 1912.*

Genealogies of an Aberdeen Family 1540-1913 by the Rev. James Smith, 4to, Aberdeen, 1913 (200).*

The Chronicles of a Puritan Family in Ireland (Smith of Glasshouse), by the Rev. G. N. Nuttall-Smith, O.U.P., 1923.*

Smith-Carington—See Carington and (above), Smith of Nottingham.

Smollett—Account of the Family of Smollett of Bonhill with a series of Letters . . . by Tobias Smollett . . . , ed. by J. Irvine, 4to, Dumbarton, 1859 (40).*

Smythie—The Records of the Smithie Family, by Major R. Raymond Smythie, 4to, London, 1912.*

Somerset—The Somerset Sequence, by Horatia Durant, London, 1951. See also Seymour.

Somerville—Memorie of the Somervilles, by James, 11th Lord Somerville, 1679; Introduction and Note by Sir Walter Scott, Bt., 2v., Edin., 1815.
The Baronial House of Somerville, comp. by J. Somerville, Glasgow, 1920.
Drum of the Somervilles, by Hamilton More Nisbett, Edin., 1928 (250).*
Records of the Somerville Family of Castlehaven and Drishane, by O. and B. T. Somerville, 1940.
See also Head.

Sorby—Genealogy of the Sorby Family, by W. H. Sorby, 1895.

Sotheran—Genealogical Memoranda relating to the Family of Sotheran of Durham . . . and to the Sept of MacManus, by Charles Sotheran, 1811; reprinted; 2 pts, 4to, London, 1871-3.

Southall—Records of the Southall Family, by C. Southall, 1932.

Southcote—The Southcote Family; Memoirs of Sir Edward Southcote, Roehampton, 1872.

Spalding—Notes and Traditions concerning the Family of Spalding, 4to, Liverpool, 1914.*

Spanton—The Spanton Family . . . , by A. T. Spanton, 4to, pamph., Hanley, 1897.

Sparks—Memoranda relating to the Sparks and Tickell Families, comp. by R. S. Boddington, 4to, 1877.*

Spedding—The Spedding Family . . . , by J. C. D. Spedding, Dublin, 1909.*

Speke—Genealogy of the Speke Family, collected by M. Pine-Coffin, fo., 1914.*
Records of the Speke Family of Jordans, by Sophia Murdoch, 4to, Reading, H. T. Morley, 1921.

Spencer—The Spencers of Bedfordshire, by J. Holding, 1903.

Spencer-Stanhope—Annals of a Yorkshire House, from the Papers of a Macaroni and his Kindred, by A. M. W. Stirling, 2v., 1911.

Spicer—Some Account of the Family of the Spicers . . . , by F. L. Spicer, Leamington, 1897.

Spottiswoode—The Spottiswoode Miscellany (from the MS. Collection of Father R. Augustine Hay), containing a Family Genealogy, ed. by James Maidment, 2v., Edin., 1844.

Spreull—Notes on the Family of Spreull, by J. M. and G. J. Spreull, Glasgow, 1915.

Spring—The Springs of Lavenham, by B. McClenaghan, 1924.

Spurgeon—The Spurgeon Family, by W. M. Higgs, 4to, 1906.

Squarey—Family Records and Pedigrees, comp. by L. M. Squarey, Salisbury, 1907.

Stafford—History of the Family of Stafford of Botham Hall, by
T. W. Stafford, n.d.

Stainton—Jane Stainton and her Family, by J. Raine, York, 1888.

Stallard—Notes and Queries . . . Name of Stallard, comp. by A. D.
Stallard, London, 1912.*

Stanford—The Descent of the Family of Stanford of Preston,
Sussex, by Charles Thomas Stanford, Chiswick Press, 1907.*

Stanhope—Notices of the Stanhopes as Esquires and Knights . . . ,
by Viscount Mahon, London, 1855.
The Stanhopes of Chevening, by Aubrey Newman, Macmillan,
1969.
See also Spencer-Stanhope.

Staniforth—Staniforthiana . . . Staniforth of Darnall, by F. M. H.,
Bristol, 1863.

Stanley—Memoires containing a Genealogical and Historical Acc-
ount of the Ancient and Honourable House of Stanley . . . ,
by John Seacombe, 4to, Liverpool, 1741: other edns., Man-
chester, 1767 and 1783, Preston, 1793, Liverpool, 1801, and
Manchester, 1821.
The History of the House of Stanley, etc., Liverpool, 1830.
The Stanley Legend . . . , by George Ormerod, Westminster,
1839.
Notes of the Noble House of Stanley, 16mo., Manchester, 1840.
Sketch of the House of Stanley and the House of Sefton, by D.
Ross, 12mo., London, 1848.
The Stanley Papers, 4to, 5v., Chetham Soc., 1853-67.
The House of Stanley, by Peter Draper, Ormskirk, 1864.
A History of the Stanleys of Knowsley, by William Pollard,
Liverpool and London, 1868-9.
The Stanleys of Alderley, by Nancy Mitford, 1968.

Stansfeld—History of the Stansfeld or Stansfield Family . . . ,
comp. by John Stansfeld, 4to, Leeds, 1885-6.*

Stapleton—The Stapletons of Yorkshire, by H. E. Chetwynd-
Stapylton, London, 1884-5 and 1897 (see Round, Peerage
and Family History, 312, et seq.).

Stapley—The Stapley Papers, comp. by Harry Stapley, London,
1905.

Starkie—The Starkie Family (parish of Leigh, co. Lancs), by
J. P. Rylands, 1880.*

Statham—The Descent of the Family of Statham, by the Rev.
S. P. H. Statham, London, 1925.

Staunton—Memoir of the Life and Family of the Late Sir G. L.
Staunton, Bt., by G. T. Staunton, Havant Press, 1823.*
The Stauntons of Staunton, Notts., by George W. Staunton
and F. M. Stenton, Newark, 1911.

Stawell—A Quantock Family . . . , ed. by Col. G. D. Stawell, 4to,
Taunton, 1910.*

Steel—See Black.

Stephen—Stephen of Linthouse 1750-1950, by J. L. Carvel, Linthouse, 1950.

Stepney—Some Notes on the Stepney Family, by R. Harrison,
London, 1870.*

Stevenson—Records of a Family of Engineers, by Robert Louis
Stevenson.
The Stevenson Family . . . , by H. S. Stevenson, 1965.

Stewart—Note: More has probably been written about the genealogy of this family than any other. For a fairly full bibliography see Margaret Stuart, Scottish Family History, Oliver and Boyd, 1930.

Memoires of the Family of the Stuarts and the Commendable Providence of God towards Them, by the Rev. John Watson, London, 1683.

A Chronological Genealogical and Historical Dissertation of the Royal Family of Stuarts, beginning with Milesius . . . , by Mathew Kennedy, LL.D., 8vo, Paris, 1705.

A Genealogical History of the Royal and Illustrious Family of Stewarts from the year 1034 . . . , by George Crawford, fo., Edinburgh, 1710. Reprinted with continuation, by W. Semple, 4to, Paisley, 1782. The same, continued by G. Robertson, 4to, Paisley, 1818.

A Genealogical and Historical Account of the Most Illustrious Name of Stuart . . . , by David Symson, Edin., 1712 and 1713.

A Short Historical and Genealogical Account of the Royal Family of Scotland from Kenneth II, with Appendix, by Duncan Stuart, 4to, Edin., 1739.

A Dissertation on the Royal Line and the First Settlers of Scotland, by Andrew Henderson, London, 1771.

A Historical Genealogy of the Royal House of the Stuarts . . . (Robert II to James VI) by the Rev. Mark Noble, 4to, 312 pp., London, Faulder, 1795.

Genealogical History of the Stewarts . . . Darnley, Lennox, and Castlemilk, by Andrew Stuart, M.P., 2v., 4to, London, 1798; supplement, 1799.

The Genealogy of the Stuarts Refuted . . . in a letter to Andrew Stuart, M.P., by Sir Henry Stuart of Allanton, Edin., 1799.

Genealogical Account of the Royal House of Stuart, 1043-1603, by Thomas Waterhouse, Grantham, 1816.

Genealogical and Historical Sketch of the Stuarts of Castle Stuart, by the Hon. and Rev. A. G. Stuart, 4to, Edin., 1854.

The Descent of the Stuarts . . . by William Townend, London, 1858; anr. edn., 1867.

The Red Book of Grandtully, by Sir William Fraser, 2v., Edin., 1868-9 (100).

La Famille des Stuarts, par E. Dubois, Rouen, 1878.

The Stewarts of Forthergill and Garth, by C. Poyntz Stewart, 4to, W. and A. K. Johnston, 1879.*

The Stewarts of Appin, by J. H. J. Stewart and Duncan Stewart, 4to, Edin., 1880.*

The Stuart Dynasty . . . , by Percy M. Thornton, London, London, 1890.

The Royal House of Stewart, by W. Gibb, with Notes by W. H. St John Hope, fo., 1890.

Some Account of the Stewarts of Aubigny, by Lady Elizabeth Cust, 4to, London, 1891 (250).

The Story of the Stewarts, by J. K. Stewart, 4to, Edin., Stewart Soc., 1901.

The Royal Stuarts, by T. F. Henderson, 1914.

The History of the Stuarts, Earls of Traquair, Barons Linton of Cabarston, and Charles Edward Stuart-Linton, by L. G. Pine, London, 1940.

Stiff—Collections relating to the Family of Stiff, by W. P. W. Phillimore, Pt. 1, London, 1892.*

Stilt—Stilt of Liverpool, by J. C. Stilt, 4to, Liverpool, D. Marples and Co., 1901.

Stirling—The Stirlings of Keir and their Family Papers, by Sir William Fraser, 4to, Edin., 1858 (150).*

Comments in Refutation of Pretensions Advanced for the First Time and Statements Made in a Recent Work, 'The Stirlings of Keir and their Family Papers', with an Exposition of the Right of the Stirlings of Drumpellier to the Representation of the Ancient Stirlings of Cadder, by J. Riddell, 4to, Edin., 1860 (300).*

The Stirlings of Craigbernard and Glorat . . . , by Joseph Bain, 4to, Edin., 1883.*

The Stirlings of Cadder . . . , ed. by G. H. Bushnell, St Andrews, 1933.

The Stirlings of Stirlingshire, Ireland, and London, by W. H. Woodward, London, 1935.

Stokes—Some Notes of the Stokes Family (cos. Wilts and Glos.), ed. by A. Schomberg, 4to, Devizes, 1909.

Stoney—Some Old Annals of the Stoney Family, comp. by F. S. Stoney, London, 1879.*

Stonor—Stonor Letters and Papers, ed. by C. L. Kingsford, 2v., Camden Soc., 1919.

Storey—Storeys of Old . . . , by R. E. K. Rigbye, 4to, Preston, 1920.

Storr—Notes on the Families of Storr of Hilston and Owstwith, by A. B. Wilson-Barkworth, Cambridge, 1890.*

Stourton—The History of the Noble House of Stourton of Stourton in Wiltshire, by Charles, Lord Mowbray, 4to, 2v., 1899 (100).*

See Round, Peerage and Family History, 1901.

Strachan—Memorials of the . . . Strachans and Family of Wise, by the Rev. Charles Rogers, 4to, London and Edin., 1873; also, 4to, 1877.*

The Strachans of Glenkindle 1357-1726, by Col. James Allardyce, 4to, Aberdeen, 1899.

Strang—Sketch of a History of the Family of Strang or Strange of Balcaskie, by William McTaggart, Edin., 1798.

Stratton—History of the Wiltshire Strattons, by James Stratton, Winchester, 1910.*

Streynsham—Notes relating to the Family of Streynsham of Fevershall, originally comp. by the Rev. G. S. Maston, 1874, with additions by Gen. Sir A. B. Streynsham, 4to, London, 1879 (18); anr. edn., 1881.*

Strickland—Sizergh Castle . . . and the Strickland Family, comp. by Lady Edeline Strickland, 4to, 1898.
The Stricklands of Sizergh Castle, by Daniel Scott, Kendal, 1908.
Genealogical Memoirs of the Family of Strickland of Sizergh . . . , by H. Hornyold, 4to, Kendal, 1928.

Strother—Records of the Family of Strother, by A. Strother, 4to, Bath, 1881.
The Strothers of Alnwick, Bilton, and Newton-on-the-Moor, by A. Strother, 4to, 1891.

Strutt—See Digby.

Stuart—See Stewart.

Stubbs—Genealogical History of the Family of Bishop William Stubbs, ed. by F. Collins, Yorks. Arch. Ass., LV., 1915.

Sturge—Family Records, by Charlotte Sturge, London, 1882.*
Annals of the Sturge Family, by Walter Sturge of Bristol, 1902.

Styring—Earls without coronets (the Styr dynasty), by H. K. Styring, 1965.

Sullivan—A Family Chronicle, derived from Notes and Letters (selected by Barbarina, Lady Grey), ed. by Gertrude Lyster, John Murray, 1908.

Sumner—Memorials of the Family of Sumner from the Sixteenth Century to 1911, 4to, 1911.*

Surtees—Records of the Family of Surtees, by Brig. Gen. H. C. Surtees and the late H. R. Leighton, 4to, Newcastle, 1925.*

Sutton—History of Dudley Castle and Priory, including a Genealogical Account of the Families of Sutton and Ward, by Charles Twamley, London, 1867.

Swinton—The Swintons of that Ilk and their Cadets, by Archibald C. Swinton, 4to, Edin., 1883;* (an earlier edn., from the Proc. Berwickshire Naturalists Club, Alnwick, 1878*).
Concerning Swinton Family Records and Portraits at Kinmerghame . . . , by A. C. and J. L. Campbell-Swinton, Edin., 1908.*

Sworder—Notes on the Family of Sworder, by T. L. Sworder, Hertford, 1910.*

Swynnerton—Account of the Family of Swynnerton of Swynnerton and Elsewhere . . . , by C. T. O. Bridgeman, London, 1886.*

Sydenham—The History of the Sydenham Family . . . , by G. F. Sydenham, ed. by A. T. Cameron, 4to, East Molesey, 1928 (300).*

Sydney—See Sidney.

Sykes—The Sykes Family, anciently of Flockton in the Parish of Thornhill . . . since of Basildon, 4to, 16pp., 1859; ? anr. edn., 1865.

Sylvester—Gens Sylvestrina . . . , by Joseph Hunter, 12mo., 1846.

Symington—Genealogy of the Symington Family, by the Rev.
    A. N. Paton, 4to, 1908.*

Symonds—On the English Family of Symonds, by J. A. Symonds,
    4to, Oxford, 1894 (100).*
  A Memoir of the Family of Symonds in Somerset and Dorset
    . . . , by Henry Symonds, Wessex Press, 1933 (50).*

Synge—The Family of Synge or Sing, comp. by Mrs L. M. Synge,
    G. F. Wilson and Co., fo., 1938.*

T

Talbot—The House of the Seals, or Memoirs of the Noble Family
    of Talbot; with the Life of Lord Chancellor Talbot, London,
    1737.
  Genealogical Memoir of the Ancient and Noble Family of Tal-
    bot of Malahide, co. Dublin, ? by Sir William Betham, fo.,
    Dublin, 1829.
  Maison des Comtes de Shrewsbury . . . , Paris, 1841.

Tate—Genealogical Record of the Tate Family, by William Tate
    of London, 4to, 1904.

Taunton—The Tauntons of Oxford, by One of Them (W. G. Taun-
    ton), 4to, London, 1902.

Taylor—The Family Pen: Memorials of the Taylors of Ongar, by
    Isaac Taylor, 2v., London, 1867.
  Some Account of the Taylor Family (originally Taylard), ed.
    by P. A. Taylor, M.P., 2v., 4to, London, 1875 (100).*
  A Memoir of the Family of Taylor of Norwich, by P. M. Tay-
    lor, Spottiswoode and Co., 1886.
  The Taylor Papers . . . Taylor of Luddenham, Darrington, and

Faversham, by G. S. Fry, ? Hove, 1923.*
The Taylors of Ongar, by D. M. Armitage, Cambridge, 1939.
Contributions towards a Bibliography of the Taylors of Ongar
and Stanford Rivers, by G. E. Harris, 1965.

Temple—Family Chronicle, Section 1a, The Temple Family, by
Lillian Clarke, Wellingborough, Perkin and Co., 1912.
The Temple Memoirs, by Col. J. T. Temple assisted by H. M.
Temple, 4to, Derby, 1925 (250).

Tennyson—The Tennysons . . . by C. Tennyson and Hope
Dyson, 1973/4.

Tennyson-D'Eyncourt—Genealogical History of the Family of
Tennyson-D'Eyncourt, by J. B. Burke, 12mo., London,
1846.

Thackeray—Memorials of the Thackeray Family, by J. T. Pryme
and A. Bayne, London, 1879 (100).*
The Thackerays in India, by Sir W. W. Hunter, 4to, 1897.

Thistlethwaite—The Thistlethwaite Family, a Study in Genealogy,
by B. Thistlethwaite, vol. 1. (all pubd), 4to, London, 1910.*

Thoms—See M'Combie.

Thomson—A Short Genealogical Account of the Family of Thom-
son in Corstorphine, Midlothian, by Alexander Deuchar,
Edin., 1816.
A History of the Family of Thomson of Corstorphine, by
T. R. Thomson, Edin., 1926 (60).*
The Thomson Family and its Pedigree, Descendants, and other
Kindred of Alexander Thomson, Greens, Monquhitter,
Aberdeenshire, and Elizabeth Clark his wife, by H. M. and
A. S. Thomson, fo., Norwich, 1896.
An Old Glasgow Family of Thomson, by G. Graham Thomson,

1903.

Thorold–Descent of the Various Branches of the Ancient Family
of Thorold, by the Ven. Edward Trollope, 4to, Lincoln,
1874.

Thrale–A New Thraliana, by Richard Thrale, St Albans,
1973.

Threipland–The Threiplands of Fingask: a Family Memoir, by
Dr Robert Chambers, 4to and 8vo, 1853; also London
and Edin., 1880-2.

Thurburne–The Thurburnes, by F. A. V. Thurburne, London,
1864.

Thursfield–Notes relating to the Family History of Thursfield,
by A. S. T., 1907.*

Thynne–Historical Account of the Family of Thynne, otherwise
Botfield, by J. Morris, Westminster, 1855.
See also Botfield.

Tickell–See Sparks.

Timperley–Timperley of Hintlesham . . . by Sir G. H. Ryan, Bt.,
and L. J. Redstone, Methuen, 1931.

Tindall–The Tindalls of Scarborough, by Christian Tindall,
Exeter, 1927.*

Tollemache–The Tollemaches of Helmingham and Ham, by
Maj. Gen. E. D. H. Tollemache, Ipswich, Cowell, 1949.

Tomkinson–Those Damned Tomkinsons, by G. S. Tomkinson,
1950 (100);* supplement, 1959.

Townsend, Townshend—An Officer of the Long Parliament and
his Descendants . . . , by R. and D. Townshend, London,
1892.

    Pedigree of the Family of Townsend . . . , ed. by R. S. Bodd-
ington, London, 1881.

    The Townshend Family, by C. H. Townshend, 1875.

    The Townshends of Raynham, by J. Durham, 1922.

Tracy—A Short Memoir, critically illustrating the Histories of the
Noble Families of Tracy and Courtenay, by John Tracy,
Canterbury, 1796.

Traill—Genealogical Account of the Traills of Orkney, by William
Traill, M.D., Kirkwall, 1883.

    Genealogical Sketches: the Frotoft Branch of the Orkney
Traills, their Relations and Connections, by T. W. Traill,
1902 (40).*

Trant—The Trant Family, by S. T. McCarthy, Folkstone, 1924;
supplement, Folkstone, ? 1927.

Travers—A Collection . . . of the Family of Travers . . . towards a
History of that Family, by S. Smith Travers, arranged by
H. J. S., Oxford, 1864 (55).

    A Pedigree of the Devonshire Family of Travers . . . , by
S. Smith Travers, arranged by Frederick B. Falkiner, 1898
(100).*

Travis—Genealogical Memorials of the Travis Family . . . , by John
Travis, Walsden, 12mo., 1893.

Treacher—Memorials of the Treacher Family; Three Generations
of a Godly House, by A. Hall, London, 1896.*

Treffgarne—A Compendium to the Ancestry . . . Treffgarne, by
W. H. Williams Treffgarne, 1932.

Tremenheere–The Tremenheeres, by Seymour Greig Tremenheere, London, H. J. Ryman, 118pp., 1922-5.*

Tregoning–Two Centuries of a Cornish Family, by E. A. Tregoning, Leicester, 1950.

Trench–Trench Pedigree; Genealogy of the Descendants of Frederick Trench of Woodlawn, by Henry Trench, fo., 1878.
A Memoir of the Trench Family, by T. R. F. Cooke-Trench, London, 1896.

Tresham–The Ruins of Liveden, with Historical Notices of the Family of Tresham, by T. Bell, 4to, London, 1847; ? reprinted 1872.

Trevor–The Trevors of Trevalyn and their Descendants, by E. S. Jones, 1955.*

Trimble–The Trimbles and Cowens of Dalston, Cumberland, by W. T. Trimble, Carlisle, Thurnam, 4to, 1935.

Tristram–Pedigree of the Family of Tristram of Belbroughton, Worcestershire, n.a., 4to, limp vellum, 1904.*

Tritton–The Place and Family, by J. Herbert Tritton, 4to, London, 1907 (150).*

Trollope–The Family of Trollope, by the Ven. E. Trollope, 4to, Lincoln, 1875.
A Memoir of the Family of Trollope, comp. by the Rev. M. N. Trollope, London, 1897.
The Trollopes, the Chronicle of a Writing Family, by L. P. and R. P. Stebbins, 1946.

Trotman–Collections relating to the Family of Trotman, by W. P. W. Phillimore, Stroud, 1892.

The Trotman Family, by F. H. Trotman, Nottingham, 1965.

Trubshaw—Family Records, by Susanna Trubshaw, 4to, Stafford, 1876.*

Tufnell—The Family of Tufnell, by E. B. Tufnell, 4to, London, 1924.*

Tufton—Memorials of the Family of Tufton, Earls of Thanet, by Robert Pocock, Gravesend, 1900.

Tupper—Family Records, by F. Brock Tupper, Guernsey, 1835.

Turing—The Lay of the Turings: A Poetical Sketch of the Family History, by H. M. M'Kenzie, 4to, 1850.*

Turner—Pedigree and Arms of the Turner Family, by Hubert Smith, ed. by R. Woof, 4to, London, 1871.*
Genealogy of the Family of Turner, comp. by S. B. Turner, 4to, London, 1884.*
The Turner Family of Mulbarton and Great Yarmouth . . . , by the Rev. Harward Turner, 4to, London, 1895; 2nd edn., enlarged by F. Johnson, 4to, 1907.*

Turton—Pedigree of Turton of Staffordshire . . . , by Frederick Augustus Homer and Cholmondeley Sherwood James, fo., London, 1924 (80).*
The Turton Family, by C. S. James, Oxford, 1927.

Tuthill—Pedigree of Tuthill of Peamore, of Kilmore, and of Faker, with Genealogical Notes of the Family, comp. by Lt. Col. P. B. Tuthill, 4to, 1908.

Tweedie, Tweedy—History of the Tweedie or Tweedy Family, by M. F. Tweedie, 4to, London, 1902.
The Dublin Tweedys, by O. Tweedy, 1956.

Twemlow–The Twemlows; their Wives and their Homes, by Col. F. R. Twemlow, 4to, Wolverhampton, 1910 (100).

Twining–Some Facts in the History of the Twining Family, by the Rev. W. H. G. Twining, 4to, London, 1892; supplement, 1893; also Salisbury, 4to, 1895.
History of the Firm and Family of Twining in the Strand, 1675-1741, by S. S. Twining, 1931.

Twisden–The Family of Twysden and Twisden . . . , by Sir J. R. Twisden, completed by C. H. Dudley Ward, Murray, 1939.

Twyman–An East Kent Family, by Frank Twyman, 1956.

Tyldesley–The Tyldesley of Lancashire . . . , by John Lunn, 1966.

Tyler–The Family History of Tyler of Gloucestershire and Bristol, by Col. J. C. Tyler, fo., Colchester, 1913.*

Tyndale–Genealogy of the Family of Tyndale, including the Family of Annesley . . . , by B. W. Greenfield, fo., London, 1843;* reprinted 8vo, 1864.

Tyrie–The Tyries of Drumkilbo, Dunnideer, and Lunan, by Andrew Tyrie, 50pp., Glasgow, 1893.

Tyrell–The Tyrells of Herm, by P. G. Lawrie, Wilson and Whitworth, 1900.*
A Genealogical History of the Tyrells . . . , by J. H. Tyrell, 4to, 1904 (100).*

Tyrwhitt–Notices and Remains of the Family of Tyrwhitt, originally seated in Northumberland at Tyrwhitt . . . , 1858; corrected and reprinted 1862-5; again by R. P. Tyrwhitt, London, 1872 (50).*

Tyttery—See Henzey.

Tyzack—See Henzey.

U

Ullathorne—Chronicle of an Ancient Yorkshire Family . . . , by
    B. L. Kentish, Kelvedon, 1963.

Underhill—The Underhills of Warwickshire, by J. H. Morrison, 4to,
    C.U.P., 1932.

Unton—The Unton Inventories, with a Memoir of the Family of
    Unton, by J. G. Nichols, 4to, London, Ashmolean Soc.,
    1841.

Unwin—Notes on the Unwin Family, by J. D. Unwin; G. Allen and
    Unwin, 1934; 2nd edn., Unwiniana, collected by P. I.
    Unwin, G. Allen and Unwin, 1937.
  The Publishing Unwins, by Philip Unwin, Heinemann, 1971/2.

Urlin—Memorials of the Urlin Family, comp. by Ethel L. H. Urlin,
    4to, 1909.

Urquhart—Μάντοχρονοχάνον , or A Peculiar Promptuary of Time:
    Wherein (not one instant being omitted since the beginning
    of motion) is displayed A most exact Directory for all
    particular Chronologies, in what Family soever: And that by
    deducing the true Pedigree and Lineal Descent of . . . the
    Urquharts, in the house of Cromartie, since the Creation
    of the World, until this present year of God, 1652. For
    Richard Baddely, 1652 (First Edition. A Notice To The
    Reader is signed G. P. The writer states that the MS. was
    saved after the battle of Worcester from the soldiers by
    an officer of Pride's regiment, and then fell by chance into
    the hands of himself, the said G. P., and that he published

the book during the author's imprisonment in the hopes of
saving his life. The writer of the notice of Sir Thomas Urquhart in the D.N.B. quotes this preface as being the author's
own composition.)

The Urquharts of Cromartie: True Pedigree and Lineal Descent
of the most Ancient and Honourable Family of Urquhart in
the House of Cromartie since the Creation of the World until
1774 (in Sir Thomas Urquhart's tracts), 12mo., Edin., 1774,
1782, etc.

The History of the Family of Urquhart, by Henrietta Tayler,
Aberdeen U. P., 1946.

Urswick—Records of the Family of Urswyck, Urswick, or Urwick,
comp. by the late T. A. Urwick, ed. by the Rev. W. Urwick,
4to, St Alban's Press, 1893.*

Usborne—Loddenden and the Usbornes of Loddenden, by H. S.
Cowper, 4to, Ashford, 1914.

Usher, Ussher—The Ussher Memoirs . . . , by the Rev. W. D. B.
Wright, 4to, Dublin, 1889.

A History of the Usher Family in Scotland, ed. by C. M. Usher,
1956.

Uvedale—Notices of the Family of Uvedale of Titsey and Wick-
ham, by G. Leveson-Gower, 1865.

V

Vachell—A Short Account or History of the Family of Vachell, by
I. and A. C. Vachell, Cardiff, 1900.*

Vaillant—The Vaillant Family, by the Rev. W. B. Vaillant, Weybridge, 1915; 2nd edn., 1928.

Vance, Vaus, Vaux—Sketch of a Genealogical and Historical Acc-

ount of the Family of Vaux, Vans, or de Vallibus; now re-
presented in Scotland, by Vans Agnew of Barnbarrow . . . ,
by V. Agnew, 4to, 36pp., Pembroke, W. E. Wilmot, 1800.
A Short Account of the Family of De Vaux, or Vaux, or
Vans of Barnbarroch, 1832.*
An Account, Historical and Genealogical of the Family of
Vance in Ireland, Vans in Scotland, anciently Vaux in Scot-
land and England, and originally de Vaux in France, by W.
Balbirnie, Cork, 1860.
Vaux of Harrowden, by G. Anstruther, Newport, 1953.

Vaughan—The Vaughans of Courtfield, by J. H. Matthews, 1912.
Genealogy of the Ancient Family of Vaughan of Tretower, by
C. Vaughan, 1940.

Venn—Annals of a Clerical Family; Family and Descendants of
William Venn of Otterton, Devon, 1600-21 by John Venn,
London, 1904; supplement, 1923.

Vere—The Fighting Veres, by Clements R. Markham, 1888.
See also de Vere.

Verney—Memoirs of the Verney Family, by Frances, Lady Verney
and ed. and completed by Margaret Maria, Lady Verney, v. 1
and 2, 1892, v. 3, 1894, v. 4, 1899; two supplementary vol-
umes, 1905-30; also a later edition.
The Verneys of Claydon . . . , by Sir H. Verney, Bt., 1968.

Vernon—Historical Memoir of the House of Vernon, by Thomas
Stapleton, 4to, 1855, unfinished, no title (100)..

Vigors—A History of the Family of Vigors, by P. D. Vigors,
1932.

Vipont—Family Records, by W. Scrutton, Bradford, 1904.*
v. 1, The Viponts, v. 2, The Ecroyds and Viponts, v. 3,

The Biltons.

Vyner—Vyner: A Family History, by C. J. Viner, 2v., 1885; supplement, 1885; revised edn., 2v., 1887.

W

Wace—The History of the Wace Family, by A. A. Wace, 1932.

Wake—A Brief Enquiry into the Antiquity . . . of the Name and Family of Wake . . . , by William Wake, Westminster, 1833 (100).

A Memoir of a Branch of the Wake Family of Northants., by H. T. Wake, Carlisle, 1861 (100).

Waldo—Notes respecting the Family of Waldo, by Morris Charles Jones, pamph., Edin., 1863-4.

Walker—Some Account of the Family of Walker of Tilehurst near Reading, comp. by Gen. G. W. Walker, R.E., for the information of Relatives, 8vo, wrappers, 35pp., Okehampton, 1906.

The Walker Family of Bolton, by A. N. Walker, 1947 (100).*

The Walker Family, Iron Founders and Lead Manufacturers 1741-1893, ed. by A. H. John, n.d.

Wallace—The Book of Wallace, by the Rev. Charles Rogers, 4to, 2v., Grampian Club, 1889 (250).

Waller—Our Family Record, by the Rev. W. A. Waller, Surbiton, Bull, 1898.

Wall—The Wall Family in Ireland, by Hubert Gallwey, Kildare, 1970.

Wallop—The Wallop Family and their Ancestry, by V. J. Watney,

4v., 4to, O.U.P., 1928 (100).*

Walpole—A Brief History of Sir Robert Walpole and Family, by W. Musgrave, London, 1732, 1738, and 1745.

Houghton and the Walpoles, by the Rev. J. H. Broome, London, 1865.

Walpole of Whaplode, being a Genealogy of the Family . . . , by W. E. Foster, Whaplode, 1889.

Mannington and the Walpoles, Earls of Orford, by Lady Dorothea Nevill, fo., Fine Arts Soc., 1894.

The Later History of the Family of Walpole of Norfolk, by Walter Rye, 1920.

Walsh—Une Famille Royaliste . . . , 4to, Nantes, 1901; translation by A. G. M. MacGregor, 4to, Edin., 1904 (320).

Walters—The Family of Walters of Dorset, Hants . . . , by F. Walters, London, 1907.*

Wandesforde—Story of the Family of Wandesforde of Kirklington and Castlecomer . . . , by H. B. M'Call, 4to, London, 1904.

Wanty—Genealogical Memoranda relating to the Family of de Vantier, anglais Wanty, by Henry Peet, 1902.*

Warburton—Memoir of the Family of Warburton of Garryhinch, Kings co., compiled at the instance of Richard Warburton, Dublin, 1848.*

The Warburtons of Arley, by J. E. Bailey, (reprint from the Papers of Manchester Literary Club), Manchester, 1881.

The Village and the Family, by Norman Warburton, London, 1970.

Ward—Notes on an old Baptist Family; Ward of Nottingham, ed. by J. T. Godfrey, Nottingham, 1900.*

See also Sutton.

Wardlaw—The Wardlaws in Scotland . . . , by John C. Gibson, 4to, Edin., 1912 (200).*

Warlow—The History of the Warlow Family with Notes on Pembrokeshire History, by G. H. Warlow, London, R. Stockwell, 1926.

Warneford—Warneford . . . , by Mary Gibson, ? 1965.

Warner—Sir Thomas Warner . . . a Chronicle of his Family, by A. Warner, West India Committee, 1933.

Warren—Memoirs of the Ancient Earls . . . of Surrey, and their Descendants of the Present Time, by the Rev. J. Watson, 4to, 1776 (6); 4to, 2v., Warrington, 1782.
A Bibliographical and Critical Account of Watson's 'Memoirs', by J. G. Nichols, 1871.
History and Genealogy of the Warren Family in Normandy, Great Britain . . . , by the Rev. Thomas Warren, 1902.*

Washbourne—The Washbourne Family, Notes and Records . . . , by G. F. Hoar, ed. by R. E. M. Peach, 4to, Gloucester, 1896.*
The Washbourne Family of Little Washbourne and Wichenford, by the Rev. James Davenport, London, 1907.

Washington—The Washington Family, by W. C. Ford, 1893.
The History of the Washington Family, by the Rev. H. Isham Longden, Northampton, 1926-7.
The Earliest Washingtons, by G. H. S. L. Washington, 1964.

Wasteneys—Some Account of Colton and the De Wasteneys Family, by the Rector and Rev. Frederick P. Parker, Birmingham, 1879.

Waterlow—Memoranda as to the Waterlow Family, by A. J. Waterlow, London, 1883.*

Watson—Rockingham Castle and the Watsons, by C. Wise, 4to,
London, 1891.
Traditions of the Watson Family, by C. B. Boog Watson, Perth,
1908.

Watt—Letters respecting the Watt Family, by George Williamson,
Greenock, 1840.*
Memoirs of the Lineage . . . of James Watt, by George William-
son, 4to, Edin., 1856.

Watts—Genealogy of the Family of Watts . . . , by W. P. W. Phillimore, Shrewsbury, 1894.*

Wauchope—History and Genealogy of the Family of Wauchope of
Niddrie-Marischal, by James Paterson, 4to, Edin., 1858.
The Ulster Branch of the Family of Wauchope, by G. M. Wau-
chope, Simkin Marshall, 1929.

Way—History of the Way Family, by Herbert W. L. Way, 4to,
1914.*
The Ways of Yesterday . . . , by A. M. W. Stirling, 1930.

Wayland—The House of Wayland . . . , 12mo., 1886.

Webb—See Richmond.

Webster—Notes Genealogical, Historical, and Heraldic, relating to
the Websters of Flamborough, London, and Warwickshire,
comp. by Capt. P. C. G. Webster, 4to, Leamington, 1880.

Wedderburn—A Genealogical Account of the Wedderburn Family,
by James Wedderburn Webster, Nantes, 1819.*
The Genealogical Account of the Wedderburn Family, by

John Wedderburn, 1824.

The Wedderburn Book . . . , by Alexander Wedderburn, 2v., 4to, 1898.

Wedgwood—The Wedgwoods, being a Life of Josiah Wedgwood . . . Memoirs of the Wedgwood and other Families, by L. Jewitt, 1865.

A History of the Wedgwood Family, by Josiah C. Wedgwood, M.P., 4to, London, 1908-9.

Wedgwood Pedigrees, by J. C. and J. G. E. Wedgwood, Kendal, 1925 and 1927.*

Welby—Notices of the Family of Welby . . . , by a Member of the Family, Grantham, 1842.*

Weld—Lulworth and the Welds, by Joan Berkeley, Gillingham, Dorset, 1971.

Wemyss—Memorials of the Family of Wemyss of Wemyss, by Sir W. Fraser, 3v., 4to, Edin., 1888 (100).

Wenham—Hastings Saga, by M. A. N. Marshall, St Catherine Press, 1953.

Wentworth—The Wentworth Genealogy, by John Wentworth, 2v., 1870.*

Branches of the Family of Wentworth, by W. L. Rutton, 4to, London, 1891 (100).

The Loyal Wentworths, by Allan Fea, London, 1928.

Werge—History of the Family of Werge, Northumberland . . . , and of Worge in Sussex, by Col. R. E. and C. E. Carr, fo., Newcastle, 1891.

Wesley—Memoirs of the Wesley Family, by Adam Clarke, London, 1823; 2nd edn., 2v., London, 1843-4.

Memorials of the Wesley Family, by G. J. Stevenson, London, 1876.

A Biographical History of the Wesley Family, by John Dove, London, 1833.

Weston—Annals of an Old Manor House (Sutton Place, Guildford), by Frederick Harrison, 4to, 1893.

West—History of our West Family of Waltham Abbey, by A. A. West, 2v., 4to, 1893-04.*

Whall—Whall of the County of Norfolk, A Family History, comp. by W. B. Whall, 4to, Taunton, 1905.

Wharton—The Whartons of Wharton Hall, by E. R. Wharton, 16mo., Oxford and London, 1898 (250).

Whatton—The Family of Whatton, a Record of Nine Centuries, by Henry W. Whatton, ed. by J. S. Whatton and W. G. D. Fletcher, London, Sylvan Press, 1929-30.

Whinyates—Family Records, by Maj. Gen. F. T. Whinyates, 3v., fo., Cheltenham, 1894-6 (25).

Whishaw—A History of the Whishaw Family, by James Whishaw, ed. by M. S. Leigh, Methuen, 1935.

Whistler—The Annals of an English Family, by the Rev. R. F. Whistler, 1887.

Whitaker—Whitaker of Hesley Hall, Grayshott Hall, Pylewell Park, and Palermo, ed. by R. S. Whitaker, 4to, London, 1907 (150).

White—The White Family of Malden, by D. P. Corry, Malden, 1878.

Memoirs of the House of White of Wallingwells . . . , Edin., 1886.

History of the Family of White of Limerick, Knockentry, Coppaghwhite . . . , by J. D. White, Cashel, 1887.

Whitehead—History of the Whitehead Families, 1200-1919, by Benjamin Whitehead, Pt. 1, Paignton, 1920.

Whitelaw—The House of Whitelaw, 1400-1900, by H. Vincent Whitelaw, Glasgow, Jackson Wylie, 1928.

Whitley—The Whitleys of Enniskillen, by T. W. Moran, 1962.*

Whitlock—A Family and a Village, by Ralph Whitlock, 1969.

Wightman—Records of the Wightman Family, by Bryan I'Anson, 1917.*

Wightwick—The Wightwicks; a Family History, comp. by H. D. Wightwick, 4to, London, W. C. Scott, 1934.

Wilder—The Wilder Family, by W. C. Wilder, 1962 (200).

Williams—Memorials of the Family of Williams, by B. Williams, Norwich, 1849.

The Family of Williams of Cowley Grove, by B. Williams, 4to, Hillingdon, 1852.*

Memorials of the Family of Williams of Cote or Coate, by B. Williams, 1904.

Willison—See Black.

Willoughby—Chronicles of the House of Willoughby de Eresby . . . , by the Hon. E. H. D. Willoughby, fo., 1896.*

The Continuation of the History of the Willoughby Family, by Cassandra Duchess of Chandos; being vol. 2 of the manuscript, ed. by A. C. Wood, Eton (Berks.), published for the University of Nottingham by the Shakespeare Head Press, 1958.

The Bizarre Barons of Rivington, by P. Willoughby-Higson, N. Briton P., 1965.

Wilmer—History of the Wilmer Family . . . , by Charles Wilmer Foster, and J. J. Green, 4to, Leeds, 1888.*

Wilson—Songs of the Wilsons, with a Memoir of the Family, ed. by John Harland, London, 1865; 2nd edn., 4to, Edin., 1866.

Pedigree of Wilson of High Wray and Kendal, by Joseph Foster, 4to, London, 1871;* 2nd edn., ed. by J. B. Foster, 4to, London, 1890.*

The Wilsons, a Banffshire Family of Factors, by A. C. Brown, Edin., 4to, 1936.

The Wilsons of Sharrow . . . , by M. F. H. Chaytor, Sheffield, 1963.

See also Carus-Wilson.

Wimberley—Memorials of the Family of Wimberley of South Witham, Beechfield, and Ayscoughfee Hall, comp. by Col. R. J. Wimberley and revised by D. Wimberley, Inverness, 1893.

Windsor—Historical Collections of the Noble Family of Windsor, by A. Collins, 4to, London, 1754.

A Monograph of the Windsor Family with a Full Account of the Coming of Age of Lord Windsor, Aug. 27, 1878, by W. P. Williams, 4to, Cardiff, 1879.

Wing—Pedigree of the Family of Wing of North Luffenham and Market Overton . . . , by E. Green, 1886.*

Wingfield—Muniments of the Ancient Saxon Family of Wing-field, by Mervyn Edward, 7th Lord Powerscourt, 4to, Lon-

don, 1894.
Some Records of the Wingfield Family, by Lt. Col. John M.
Wingfield, John Murray, 1925-6.

Winkley—Documents relating to the Winkley Family, by William
Winkley junr., Harrow, 1863.*

Winnington—Familia Wynyngtonorum, printed by Sir Thomas
Phillipps for Sir Thomas Winnington, fo., n.d. (20).

Wise—See Strachan.

Wishart—Life of George Wishart . . . and a Genealogical History of
the Family of Wishart, by the Rev. Charles Rogers, Edin., and
London, Grampian Club, 1876.
Genealogical History of the Wisharts of Pittarrow and Logie
Wishart, by G. D. Wishart, 77pp., Perth, 1914.

Wither—Materials for a History of the Wither Family, by the
Rev. R. F. Bigg-Wither, 4to, Winchester, 1907 (200).

Withie—Pedigree of the Family of Withie, by F. G. Lee, D.D.,
1880.

Withypoll—The Family of Withypoll, by G. C. Moore Smith, revised with additions by P. H. Reaney, 4to, Walthamstow Antiq
Soc., 34, 1936.

Wodehouse—The Wodehouses of Kimberley, by John, Earl of Kimberley, 1887.*

Wolfe—The Wolfes of Forenaghts, . . . , co. Kildare
. . . by Lt. Col. R. T. Wolfe, 1885; 2nd edn.,
Guildford, 1893.

Wollaston—Genealogical Memoirs of the Elder and Extinct Line of the Wollastons of Shenton and Finborough, by R. E. Chester Waters, 4to, London, 1877 (35).*

Wood, Woodd—A Family Record, or Memoirs of Basil Woodd and of Several Deceased Members of His Family, 12mo., London, 1834.

Memorials of the Family of Wood of Largo, ed. by Mrs F. M. Montagu, 4to, 1863.

Pedigree and Memorials of the Family of Woodd of Shynwood, Salop, and Brize Norton, Oxon., and of the Family of Jupp of London and Wandsworth, by C. H. L. Woodd and George Harrison, 4to, London, 1875.*

Genealogical, Heraldic, and other Records . . . Family of Woodd formerly of Shynewood, by Henry Woodd, 4to, London, 1880-6.*

Pedigree of Wood of Leicester, by H. J. Roby, Manchester, 1890.

The Wood Family of Burslem . . . , by F. Falkner, 4to, 1912 (450).*

Woodcock—Woodcock of Cuerden, Newburgh and of Wigan, by A. E. P. Gray, 4to, Canterbury, 1882.*

Woodgate—A History of the Woodgates of Stonewall Park and Summerhill, by the Rev. G. and G. M. G. Woodgate, Wisbech, 1910.*

Woodroffe—Pedigree of Woodroffe of Plusterwine . . . , by R. Hovenden, 4to, 1876 (50).*

Pedigree of Woodroffe with Memorials and Notes, collected by S. M. Woodroffe, 4to, London, 1878 (130).*

Wordsworth—Genealogical Memoranda relating to the Family of Wordsworth, by E. J. Bedford, 4to, London, 1881 (50).*

The Wordsworths of Peniston, by G. G. Wordsworth, 1929.

Worthington—Short History of the Worthington and Jukes Families, by P. W. L. Adams, 1902.*

Wray—History of the Wrays of Glentworth, Lincs., with Appendix, by Charles Dalton, 2v., London and Aberdeen, 1880-1.
The Wrays of Donegal, by C. V. Trench, O.U.P., 1945.

Wreford—Records and Pedigrees of the Wreford Family of Devonshire, by G. Wreford, 4to, n.d.; 2nd edn., revised and extended, 4to, 1909.*

Wren—Parentalia, or Memoirs of the Family of Wren, by Stephen Wren, fo., London, 1750; later edn., by Ernest J. Enthoven, fo., Sussex House Press, 1903 (250); facsimile copy, with extra illustrations, The Heirloom, 1965.
An Account of the Family of Wren of Binchester . . . , by John Thompson, 4to, Bishop Auckland, 1902.

Wrightson—Memorials of the Family of Wrightson, by W. G. Wrightson, London, 1894.

Wyat, Wyatt—The Family of Wyat, by R. S. Boddington, London, ? 1877.
Genealogical Information relating to Richard Wyatt . . . Almshouses at Godalming . . . , by E. B. Jupp, 4to, and 8vo, n.d. (150).*

Wyncoll—The Wyncolls of Suffolk and Essex, by Col. C. E. Wyncoll, Colchester, 1911.*

Wyndham—A Family History, by the Hon. H. A. Wyndham, vol. 1, 1410-1688, O.U.P., 1939; vol. 2, 1688-1837, O.U.P., 1950.

Wynne—The History of the Gwydir Family, by Sir John Wynn, first published by the Hon. D. Barrington, London, 1770; with Introduction and Notes by A Native of the Principality

(Miss A. Lloyd), 4to, Oswestry, 1818, and 4to, Ruthin, 1827; 2nd edn., etc., as Wynnstay and the Wynns, a Volume of Varieties, put together by the Author of the 'Gossiping Guide to Wales' (Askew Roberts), 4to, Oswestry, 1876, 1878, and 1885; also, with an Introduction by J. Bullinger, Cardiff, 1927.

See also Kenrick.

Y

Yardley—Pedigree of the Family of Yardley of Chatham, comp. by William Brigg, London, 9pp., 1891.*

Yarker—The Genealogy of the Surname of Yarker, by John Yarker, 4to, Manchester, 1882.*

Yarner—Collections concerning the Family of Yarner, co. Wicklow, by Col. — Houghton, 1870.*

Yea—History of the Family of Yea, by A. J. Monday, Taunton, 4to (25), and 8vo, 1885.

Yelverton—A Complete Account of the Yelverton Family, 1861.

Yerburgh—Some Notes on the Family History, by E. R. Yerburgh, 4to, London, 1912.

Young—A Genealogical Account of the Descendants of James Young, Merchant Burgess of Aberdeen, and Rachel Cruickshank, his Wife, 1697-1893, by Alexander Johnston, 4to, Aberdeen, 1861 and 1894 (125).

Histories of the Families of Young and Goodall (Isle of Wight), by Sidney Young, London, 1913.*

The Young Family of Bristol, by W. J. Young, 1937.

Younger—Account of the Family of Younger, co. Clackmannan,

by the Rev. A. W. C. Hallen, Edin., 4to, 1890.*
Account of the Family of Younger (Dumfries and Peebles) by
the Rev. A. W. C. Hallen, Edin., 4to, 1890.
The Younger Centuries 1749-1945, by David Keir, Edin., 1951.

Younghusband—Notes on the Family of Younghusband of Northumberland, by R. W. Twigge, London, 1877.*

Yvery—A Genealogical History of the House of Yvery in its Differ-
ent Branches of Yvery, Luvel, Perceval, and Gournay . . . , by
J. Anderson and William Whiston, 2v., London, 1742* (original
Introduction 41pp., revised Introduction 36pp.)
An Epitome of the Genealogical History . . . by J. Anderson,
30pp., 1747.
The House of Yvery, by John Perceval, 2nd Earl of Egremont,
1764 (noted by Malone as 'printed but not published').

ADDENDA

A

Acland—A Devon Family: the Story of the Aclands, by Anne Acland, 1980.

Acton—The Actons, by Peter Gunn, 1978.

Adams—The Adamses of Lidcott, by H.S. Tog, 1969.
The Adams Family of Kilcreen, by John Adams, U.S.A., 1974.

Adkins—The Adkins Family of South Northamptonshire and North Oxfordshire, compiled by Barbara Ann Adkins, 1968.

Airlie—The House of Airlie, by W. Wilson, 2 vols., 1924.

Alliston—Pedigrees of Alliston and Elliston of Essex and Kent, n.d.

Angus—The Baronage of Angus and Mearns. Comprising the Genealogy of three hundred and sixty families . . . D. MacGregor Peter, Edinburgh, 1856.

Antrobus—Pedigree of Antrobus extracted from the Records of the Heralds' College, fol., London, 1969.

Armstrong—The Armstrong Borderland, by W.A. Armstrong, 1960.
The History of Armstrong, by W.R. Armstrong, Pittsburgh, Penn., 1969.

Arnold—Poets and Historians: a Family Inheritance, by Mary

Moorman, Tennyson Research Centre, Lincoln, 1974.
The Arnolds, by M. Trevor, 1973.

Atwater–History and Genealogy of Atwater, by Francis Atwater, 1901.

Auerbach–The Auerbach Family, by S.M. Auerbach, 1965.

Austin–An Old Colonial Family 1685-1900, by Dora P. Burslem and Audrie D. Manning, [Evesham], 1973.*

Averenches–Pedigree of the Families of Averenches and Crevequer, by J. Renton Dunlop, 1927.

B

Bacon–The Bacon Family, by J.B. Grimston, Earl of Verulam, 1961.

Bagot–Memorials of the Bagot Family, by Lord Bagot, 4to., Blithfield, 1824.
History of the Family of Bagot . . . by Maj.-Gen. the Hon. G. Wrottesley, 1908. [Reprinted from The Staffordshire Collections, William Salt Society, Vol. XI, New Series.]

Bannerman–Bannerman of Elsick, by Donald Bannerman, Edinburgh, 1974.*

Barclay–Uncommon People, by P. Bloomfield, 1955.

Barnard–In Search of Ann: Some Fragments of a Family Genealogy, by R.A. Parker, 1974.

Barraud–Barraud: The Story of a Family of Artists and Craftsmen, by E.M. Barraud, 1967.

Bartlett—The Marlin Compound, by F.C. Oltorf, 1968.

Barry—Etude sur l'histoire des Bary-Barry, [by] C. de Barry, 1927.
De l'origine des Barry d'Irlande, [by] A. de Bary, 1900.

Baylay—Notes about Baylays and Their Pictures, by J. Baylay, 1910.

Bayntun—Notes on the Bayntun Family, edited by Hylton Bayntun-Coward, sm. fol., 1977.*

Bazeley—Pedigree of the Family of Bazely of Dover, by Mrs L. Bazely, 1909.

Beakbane—Beakbane of Lancaster: A Study of a Quaker Family, compiled by Renault Beakbane, illustrated . ... by W. Robin Jennings, Kidderminster, 1977.

Beauclerk—The House of Nell Gwyn, the Fortunes of the Beauclerk Family 1670-1974, by Donald Adamson and Peter Beauclerk Dewar, London, 1974.

Beazley—Pedigree of the Family of Beazley, by F.C. Beazley, 1921.

Behn—The Behn Family in Australia, by Ervyn C. Behn and Henry C. Behn, Australia, 1979.

Belasyse—Inwell Beware: The Story of Newburgh Priory and the Belasyse Family 1145-1977, [by] Geoffrey Ridsdill Smith, Kineton, 1978.

Bentley—Double Thread: The Chronicle of a Family 1725-1970, [by] Muriel M. Stevens, 1971.*

Benzies—A Benzies Inheritance 1260-1695, [by] Culross, 1977.

Beresford—The Book of the Beresfords, by Hugh de la Poer Beresford, Chichester, 1977.

Bickersteth—Ancient Charters and Documents Relating to Lands at Aughton, in the Hundred of West Derby in Lancashire, 4to., n.d.*

Bingham—Peers and Plebs: Two Families in a Changing World, by Madeleine Bingham, London, 1975.

Bingley—Bingley, An English Family Notebook, by Randall Bingley, Orsett Heath, Essex, 1978.* (400).

Birch—The Family of Birch of Birch near Manchester, by H. Birch, 1900.

Blackmore—The Blackmore Papers, edited by R. Brook Aspland, (?1975).

Blofeld—An Account of the Blofeld Family of Hoverton House, Norfolk, by G. Blofeld, London, 1978.*

Bolton—The Family of Theophilus Bolton of Clevedon, Somerset, and possibly Dublin, by Herbert Cairns Bolton, n.d.

Bonville—See Pole.

Bonython—The Histories of the Families of Bonython of Bonython and Bonython of Carclew, by E.G. Bonython, 1966.*

Booty—Some Bootys and their Forebears, by Harold Booty, Guildford, 1976.* (300).

Bourchier—Records of a Clerical Family, by H.S. Eeles, 1959.

Bourne—The Bourne(s) Families of Ireland, by M.A. Strange, U.S.A., 1970.

Bowater—Pedigree of Sir Edward Bowater, by A.W. Woods, 4to., 1875.*

Bradford—A Miscellany of Ancestors, by David Henry Cozens, Bideford, 1973.

Bradley—Bradley and Hughes of Belgrave. With an Appendix on Tyler of Quenborough, by J.E.O. Wilshere, 4to, 1966.

Braithwaite—The Braithwaite Clan: A Sequel to 'Generoso germine gemmo': a genealogical study, by G.E. Braithwaite, Ledbury, 1974.

Brett—Long Shadows Cast Before: Nine Lives in Ulster, 1625-1977, [by] C.E.B. Brett, Edinburgh, 1978.

Bright—The Brights of Suffolk, by J.B. Bright, Boston, U.S.A., 1858.
Notes on the Hallamshire Family of Bright, by W.S. Porter, 1897.

Bronte—In the Steps of the Brontes, by E. Raymond, 1971.
Bronteana, by J.H. Turner, 1898.

Brooke—The Brimming River, by R.F. Brooke, 1961.

Brooksby—The Brooksby Family, by Emmeline Garnett, Frisby-on-the-Wreake, 1979.

Brydon—See Gurney.

Budge–The History and Genealogy of the Budge Family of
          Trotternith Skye, by Eleanor M. Budge, Dunvegen, 1975.*

Buxton–Family Sketchbook, by E.E. Buxton, 1964, 1968.

Byron–The Byrons and Trevanions, [by] A.L. Rowse, London,
          1978.

C

Cabell–The Cabells and Their Kin, by Alexander Brown, U.S.A.,
          1939.

Cameron–John Cameron, Non-Juror, His Ancestors and Descend-
          ants . . . [Cameron of Worcester], by G.H. Cameron, 4 parts,
          Oxford, 1919-23.*
       The Camerons, a History of the Clan Cameron, by John Stewart
          of Advorlich [Glasgow], 1974.

Campion–The Family of Edmund Campion, by Leslie G.
          Campion.

Cantwell–A Cantwell Miscellany, by B.J. Cantwell, 1960.

Carew–Combat and Carnival, by P. Carew, 1954.
       A Cornish Chronicle, by F.E. Halliday, 1967.

Carey–The Careys [by] Honor Rudnitzky, Belfast, 1978.

Carne–The Carne Family of Nash Manor, Glamorgan County
          Records, 1952.

Carr-Harris–The Carr-Harris History and Genealogy, by G. Carr-
          Harris, 1966.

Carter–The Carters of King's Langley, [by] Robert Humphrey,

King's Langley, [1978].

The Carters of Virginia: Their English Ancestry, by Noel Currer-Briggs, 1979.

Cartland—The Irish Cartlands and Cartland Genealogy, by Sir George and John Barrington Cartland, [Bromsgrove, 1978].*

Cawston—Echoes of the Good and Fallen Angels, De Cawston, Norfolk, by L.B. Behrens, Battle, 1956.

Cecil—The Later Cecils, by Kenneth Rose, London, 1975.

Charles—Our Family History, by Canon J.H. Charles, Bournemouth, 1935.

Charley—Romance of the Charley Family, by I.H. Charley, 1970.

Cheyney—See Wyatt.

Child—Some Account of the Child Family, 1550-1861, written and illustrated by Kenneth Child, Chichester, 1974.

Chitty—Chitty of London, by Erik Chitty, Harrow, 1975.*

Cholmley—The Abbey House, Whitby, under the Cholmley Family, by F.R. Pearson, Whitby, Yorks., 1954.
Letters and Papers of the Cholmeleys from Warnfleet, by G.H. Cholmeley, 1964.

Christian—The Yesterday behind the door, by S.E. Hicks Beach, Liverpool, 1956.

Churchill—The Churchills, by Kate Fleming, London, 1975.
The Churchills: Portrait of a Great Family, by John Watney, London, 1977.

Climo—The Chronicle of the Climo Family in New Zealand, New Zealand, (?1979).

Clitherow—Boston Manor and the Clitherow Family, by A.J. Howard, 1969.

Colebrook—The Family of William Colebrook, by G.M. Stanford, T.P.R. Layng, 1969.

Collyer Fergusson—See Fergusson.

Comber—Comber: The Story of a Family, by G.B. Barrow, [1980].

Conquest—Story of a Theatre Family, by F. Fleetwood, 1952/3.

Conwy—Bodrhydden and the Families of Shipley-Conwy and Rowley-Conwy, by N. Tucker, 1963.

Cooke—The Seize Quartiers of the Family of Bryan Cooke Esq. of Owston, Hafod-y-Wern and Gwysanty . . . by Wm. Bryan Cooke, 4to, 1857.*
   Genelaogical Memoranda Relating to the Family of Cooke of Kingsthorp etc., 4to, 1873.*

Couchman—Couchman. Some Notes and Observations on the Antiquity and Origin of the Above Name, by C. Couchman, Coulsden, 1968.*

Coward—Coward-Slekton i England og Norge [The Coward Family in England and Norway], by Dag Coward, Bergen, 1979.

Cox—The Cox's of Craig Court, by K.R. Jones, 1969.

Coy—Family History of Coy and O'Coy, by John Robert Peter Coy, Birmingham, 1977.

Cranmer—Genealogical Memoirs of the Kindred Families of Thomas Cranmer, Archbishop of Canterbury and Thomas Wood, Bishop of Lichfield, by Robert Edmond Waters, Robson, 1877.

Crevequer—See Averenches.

Crioll or Kyriell—Pedigree of the Family of Crioll or Kyriell, by J. Renton Dunlop, 1927.

Cromartie—The Earls of Cromartie, their Kindred, Country, and Correspondence, by Sir William Fraser, 2 vols, 4to, Edinburgh, 1876.

Cruden—The Cruden Family Tree—Children and Grandchildren of William Cruden (Gravesend) 1733-1809, n.d.

Cubitt—Robert Cubitt of Bacton, Norfolk (1713-1790) and his Cubitt Descendants. Second edition, by G.E.S. Cubitt, 1963.

Cull—Directory of Male Persons of the Name of Cull, by L. Cull, 1973.

Cullwick—Notes on the Genealogy of the Cullwick Family, by E.G. Culwick, n.d.

Cunliffe—See Sparling.

Cunningham—Galloway Ancestors Revisited, by Drew McClamroch Landsborough, Thornton Heath, 1978.*

Cutler—John Cutler and his Descendants, a Partial Genealogy, by John M. Cutler, London, 1973.

Cutler—John Cutler and his Descendants, by J.M. Cutler, 1973.

D

Danforth—The Home of Nicholas Danforth in Framlingham, Suffolk, by J. Booth, 1954.

Darby—The Darbys and the Ironbridge Gorge, by Brian Bracegirdle [and] Patricia H. Miles, Newton Abbot, 1974.

Darwin—Pedigree of the Family of Darwin, by H.F. Burke, 1888 (60).*

Davies—North Country Bred: A Working Class Family Chronicle, by C.S. Davies, 1963.

Day—Family Papers, edited by Samuel H. Day, 4to, 1911.*

Deeley—The Deeley Family of Launton and Arncott, Oxfordshire, compiled by Barbara Atkins, Banbury, 1970.

Delafield—The Pedigree and Arms of Delafield, folio, 1925.*

De La Rue—The House that Thomas Built: the Story of De La Rue, by L. Houseman, 1968.

Delavals—Those Delavals, by R. Burgess, 1972.

Demain—Some Notes on the Family of Demain or Demaine, by J.R.H. Greeves, 1949.

Denham—The Denham Family, by V. and C.H. Denham, Detroit, 1940.

Derwentwater—Northern Lights, the Story of Lord Derwentwater, by R. Arnold, 1959.

Devenish—Records of the Devenish Families, by B.T. Devenish and

C.H. MacLaughlin, 1948.

Dickinson—Winging Westward from Eton dungeon to Millfield Desk, by Joy Burden, Bath, 1974.

Dixon—The James, Pyne, Dixon Family Book, compiled by Alicia C. Percival, London, 1977.*

Donaldson—Donaldson: A History of the William Donaldson Family of St. Andrews, Fife, Scotland [and] his Descendants in the United States of America, by Patricia Donaldson, Ohio, 1978.

Doncaster—The Story of Four Generations 1778-1938, by D. Doncaster, 1938.

Dougall—James Dougall of Glasgow (1699-1760) and his Descendants in the United States and Canada, by Richardson Dougall, U.S.A., 1973.

Doveton—The Dovetons of St. Helena, by E. Carter, Cape Town, 1973.

Drage—Family Story, by C. Drage, 1969.

Drysdale—The Drysdales, by D.C.L. Drysdale, Pevensey Bay, 1978.*

Durtnell—From an Acorn to an Oak Tree: a Study in Continuity, [by] C.S. Durtnell [New Edition], 1975.

Dwynn—The Dwynns of South Wales, by T.W. Newton Dunn, Devizes, 1954.*

E

Elford—The Elford's: the Story of an Ancient English Family researched and compiled by Laura Elford, Camborne, [1976].*

Elliott–The Elliots: the Story of a Border Clan, by Lady Dora Eliot, London, 1974 (950).*

Elliston–See Alliston.

Eure–Pedigree of Eure, of Easby, Ingleby, Malton &c., Yorkshire, and of Witton, Co. Durham. Reprinted from The Visitation of Yorkshire of 1584/5 &c., edited by Joseph Foster, 1875.*

Eustace–The Eustaces of the Chiltern Hundreds, by Donald W. Eustace, London and Boston, 1974.*
Part 2, London, 1979.*

Evers–Butterflies in Camphor, A Family Chronicle, by Elliot Evers, London, The Research Publishing Co., 1974.

Eyre–Signpost to Eyrecourt: Portrait of the Eyre Family Triumphant in the Cause of Liberty; Derbyshire, Wiltshire, Galway c. 1415-1856, by Ida Gantz, Bath, 1975.

F

Fairhead–The Fairhead series I to X, [by] A.E. Fairhead, [Norwich,] [1976].

Farnham–Farnham Descents from Henry III and the Subsequent Kings of England, 3 parts, 4to, Cavan, 1860.*

Feilding–The Feilding Album, by Lady W. Elwes, 1950.

Fergusson–Genealogical Memoranda Relating to the Families of Fergusson and Colyer Fergusson, 1897.*

Fetherstonhaugh—Uppark and Its People, by M. Meade-Fetherston-
haugh and M.W.O. Warner, 1964.

Finch—Jane Finch and Her Family, by Jane and John Finch,
Worthing, 1974.*

Fisher—The Search for Ann Fisher, by Florence Fisher, London,
1975.

Fitz-Gerald—The Knights of Glin, a Geraldine Family, by J.
Anthony Gaughan, Dublin, 1978.

Fitzwalter—Scotland's Lost Royal Line: the Descendants of
Duncan II, Dumfries, 1957.

Fletcher—The Fletcher House of Lace, and its Wider Family
Associations, Derby, 1957.
Notes for the Pedigree of Fletcher, by W.P. Fletcher, 1954.
See also Longridge.

Florey—The Floreys of Standlake, by Mrs. J. Goadby, Oxford,
1974.

Flower—The Flowers of Wiltshire, compiled by Mary Flower,
London, 1979.

Flowers—Some Notes on a Portsmouth Branch of the Flowers
Family 1793-1974, by A.A.M.-G. Mauleverer and R.A.
Gardiner, East Moseley, 1974.

Ford—Gathering up the Threads. A Study in Family Biography,
by F.A. Keynes, 1950.

Forster—See Foster.

Forsyth—Short Notes on the Family of Forsyth [by A.C.W.

Forsyth], [Arbroath, 1977].*

Foster—A Pedigree of the Forsters and Fosters of the North of England . . . by Joseph Foster, 4to, 1871.*
The Royal Descents of the Fosters of Moulton, and the Mathesons of Shinness and Lochalsh, by W.E. Foster, 1912.

Foster Barham—The Foster Barham Genealogy, by F. Foster Barham, 1844.*

Fowke—The Fowkes of Boughrod Castle, by E. and H. Green, 1973.

Francklin—The Francklin Family of Sturry, Canterbury and Chislet, by Thomas Sloper Church, [1978?].

Franklyn—Short Genealogical and Heraldic History of the Families of Franklyn, Beckenham, 1932.

Fraser—The Clan Fraser of Lovat, by C.I. Fraser, 1966.
Avenue of Ancestors, by A.C. Maxwell and J. Bridgeman, 1966.

French—County Records of the Surnames of Francus, Franceis, French, in England, 1100-1350, by A.D. Weld French, Boston, U.S.A., 1896.*

Frere—Frere of Suffolk and Norfolk, by J.G. Frere, 1965.

Fry—Can You Find Me? A Family History, [by] Christopher Fry, O.U.P., 1978.

G

Gamgee—The Remarkable Gamgees, a Story of Achievement, by Ruth D'Arcy Thomson, Edinburgh, 1974.

Gammell–The Gammells of Greenock and afterwards of Drumtochy, Count Esswells and Ardiffery and now of Alrick, by E.B. Gammell, [1978?].

Geraldine–The Geraldines, an Experiment in Irish Government, by B. Fitzgerald, 1951.
The Meath Geraldines, by H.J. Gerrard, 1965.

Ghent–The Continental Origins of the Ghent Family of Lincolnshire, by Richard M. Sherman, [Lincoln, 1978].

Gibbs–The Gibbs Family of Aylesbury, by C.F. Reynolds, Uxbridge, 1979.

Gilbert–The Canal Pioneers, by R.M. and H.E.P. Larking, Goring-by-Sea, 1979.*

Gilbey–Merchants of Wine, by A. Waugh, 1957.

Gilbreth–Belles on Their Toes, by F.B. Gilbreth and E.G. Carey, 1950.

Gladstone–The Gladstones, by S.G. Checklands, 1971.

Glazebrook–Notes on the Glazebrooks of Nottinghamshire, by C.J. Glazebrook, Northampton, 1974.*
Descendants of the Glazebrooks, by C.J. Glazebrook, Northampton, 1974.*
Descendants of the Glazebrooks of Madeley, Shropshire, compiled by C.J. Glazebrook, Northampton, 1974.*

Goadby–The Goadby Family 1550-1974: 25 folding chart pedigrees and notes compiled by R.R.L. Goadby, 1975.

Goddard–Documents Relating to the Goddard Family, by A.W. Mabbs, 1960.

Goldney—Goldney: a House and a Family, by P.K. Stembridge, 1969.

Gordon-Lennox—Goodwood, by David Hunn, London, 1975.

Gorges—The Story of a Family through Eleven Centuries, by R. Gorges, 1944.

Gower—The Descendants of Roger Gower, by D. Gamble, 1897.

Grazebrook—The Family of Grazebrook: Genealogical Memoranda, by C. Grazebrook, 4to, 1878.*
Pedigree of the Family of Grazebrook since their Settlement at Shenston, Co. Stafford, in 1204, by G. Grazebrook, 4to, 1899.

Greig—Greig and his Scottish Ancestry, by J.R. Greig, 1952.

Grey—The Greys of Bradgate, written by Joan Stevenson, Leicester, 1976.

Griffiths—Griffiths was their Name, by Dorothy P. Young, 1976.

Grubb—The Grubbs of Tipperary, by G.W. Grubb, Cork, 1972.

Gunning—The Pastel Portrait: the Gunnings of Castle Coote and Howards of Hampstead, by I. Gantz, 1963.

Gurney—Gurney, 1800-1965; Brydon, 1837-1965, Family History, compiled . . . by Gladys E.G. Lichtenwalter, [1975?].
The Northrepps Grandchildren, by Verily Anderson, Lavenham, 1979.
The Intwood Story, by A.J. Nixstaman, 1972.

Gwydir—History of the Gwydir Family . . . First Published by the Hon. Daines Barrington . . . now re-edited [by Miss A.

Llwyd] , 4to, Ruthin, 1827.
History of the Gwydir Family, by Sir John Wynne, Oswestry,
1878.

Gwysaney—A Genealogical History of the House of Gwysaney, by
J.B. Burke, 4to, 1847.*

Gye—A History of the Gye Family, by Peter Hadley, Helston,
1979.

B

Haddington—Memorials of the Earls of Haddington, by Sir
William Fraser, 2 vols, 4to, Edinburgh, 1889 (150).

Hadley—A Hadley History, by Peter Hadley, 1978.

Haggard—Too Late for Tears, by Lilias Rider Haggard, n.d.

Hakes—The Hakes Family, by H. Hakes, Second Edition with
additions, U.S.A., 1889.

Hall—Notes on the Surname of Hall, by G.W. Marshall, 1887.*
Hall Formerly of Nottingham and Whatton Manor, by J.G.
Corbett, Fareham, 1976.

Halsted—Of Yeoman Stock: the Halsteds of Rowley, by Leslie
Chapples, Farnham, 1978.*

Hamilton—Memorials of the Earls of Haddington, by Sir William
K. Fraser, Edinburgh, 4to, 1899 (150).*

Hamley—The Hamley, Hambey, Hamlyn Group of Families:
Historical and Genealogical Notes, compiled by Douglas
W. Hamley, Norwich, [1977] .*

Hammond–The Hammonds of Edmonton, by J.G.L. Burnby, Enfield, 1973.

Hannay–The Hannays of Sorbie, by Stewart Francis, London, 1977.

Hanscombe–Common Blood: an Exercise in Family History, by C.E. Hanscom, 1967.

Hardy–The Early Hardys, by F.R. Southerington, 1968.

Harlakenden–Pedigree of Harlakenden: 'Harlakenden' in Woodchurch, Kent and of 'Ufton' in Turnstall, n.d.

Harmer–Harmer of Sussex, by S.J. Harmer, Birmingham, 1972.*

Harrington–Harrington Family Miscellany, by D. Harrington, 1975.

Harris–Harris Annals, by Mary Tindall Collins, Fordingbridge, 1973.

Harrison–Pedigree of the Family of Harrison, with Notices of Several Members of the Family, by W.J. Cripps, 4to, 1881.*

Hasted–See Ray.

Hawks–See Longridge.

Head–The Heads of Winterbourne and Newbury, Berks, by L.G.H. Horton-Smith, 1946.

Heathcote–The Heathcote Family 1580-1924, by Charles William Heathcote, 1924.

Heffernan–The Heffernans and Their Times, by P. Heffernan,

1940.

Heigham—See Ray.

Hemingway—At the Hemingways: a Family Portrait, by M.H. Sanford, 1963.

Henry—The Descendants of Philip Henry M.A., by Sarah Lawrence. Facsimile reprint of 1844 edition.

Hickman—The Hickmans of Oldswinford, by M.V. Herbert, London, 1979.

Hodgkin—The Hodgkin Pedigree Book, or Dates of Births, Marriages and Deaths of the Hodgkin Family 1644-1906, 4to, 1907.*

Hodsoll—Wills and Other Records Relating to the Family of Hodsoll, by J. Greenstreet, 1881.

Hoffmeister—A Growing Tree: A History of the Hoffmeister Family of Portsmouth and Cowes 1781-1918, by Philip Aubrey, Camberley, 1978.*

Holles—Memorials of Holles 1493-1656, by Gervase Holles, edited from the MSS. at Longleat and Welbeck, by A. C. Ward, 4to, Camden Soc. Vol. 55, 1937.

Hollis—See Larcom.

Hooper—See Rawlins.

Hopwood—A History of Hopwood Hall, by C.S. MacDonald, 1963.

Houghes—In Search of Angelsey [sic] Ancestry, by Elizabeth

Grace Roberts, Liverpool, 1973.*

Housman—Bromsgrove and the Housmans, by John Pugh, Bromsgrove, 1974 (100).*

Hovenden—Pedigree of the Family of Hovenden . . . England, Showing the Descendants in England and U.S.A., compiled by R. Hovenden, 1908.*

Howard—Indication of Memorials, Monuments, Paintings and Engravings of Persons of the Howard Family . . . by H. Howard, folio, 1834.*
Luke Howard, his Ancestors and Descendants, 1949.

Hughes—In Search of Ancestry, by E.G. Roberts, 1973.
See also Bradley.

Hunloke—The Hunlokes of Wingerworth Hall, by David G. Edwards, Second Edition, Chesterfield, 1976.*

Hunter—Brother Surgeons, by G. Rogers, 1957.

I

Imbert—Les Imbert. The Chronicle of an Ancient Family, written and compiled . . . by Sir H.M. Imbert-Terry Bart., 1930.*

J

James—Pedigree of James and Grevis James of Ightham Court, by E. Green and T.C. Fergusson, 1912.
The James, Pyne, Dixon Family Book, compiled by Alicia C. Percival, 1977.

Jamieson—For Generations Yet Unborn: the Jamieson Family 1747-1978, by Kingsley Ireland. 1979?

Jarrom—The Evolution of the Family of Jarrom and Jerram, by
   Col. E.J. Jerram, 4to, 1965.*

Jeffs—The Jeffs Families of Northamptonshire, by L.D. Jeffs,
   1973.

Jermy—A Brief History of the Jermy Family of Norfolk and
   Suffolk, by Stewart Valdar, [New Edition] , 1976.*

Jerram—See Jarrom.

Johnson—The Johnsons of Tidmington . . . by P. Drinkwater,
   Shipton-on-Stour, 1978.*

Jones—The Pedigree of the Family Jones of Berkshire, Wiltshire,
   London and Other Places, from 1795 to Date, compiled by
   K.B. Jones, 1974.
   The Jones Family of Launton, Oxfordshire, compiled by
   Barbara Adkins, Banbury, 1973.
   The Family History of Thomas Jones the Artist, by R.C.B.
   Oliver, 1970.
   Jones (of Brawdey) English and Welsh Genealogy through
   Thirty Generations, by B.H. Clapcott, n.d. (?1975).
   Notes on the Jones Family of Bermuda, by L.P. Jones, 1947.

Judkins—A Short History of Judkins, by W.H. Collidge, 1966.

K

Kaulback—The Kaulbacks, by Roy James Alfred Kaulback,
   London, 1979.*

Kay—A Record of the Kay Family of Bury, Lancashire in the
   17th and 18th Centuries [also Darbishire and Gaskell] , by
   G.M. Ramsden, Horsham, 1978.

Keats—Thomas Hardy's Neighbours, by E.A. Last, 1969.

Keith—The Keith Book, by A.K. Merrill, 1934.

Kennedy—The Kennedys 'Twixt Wigton and the Toon of Ayr, by Sir J. Fergusson, 1958.

Kenrick—Kenricks in Hardware, a Family Business: 1791-1966, by R.A. Church, 1969.

Kennett—The Kennett Family: Pedigree of the Kennett Family, Mitre, n.d.

Kenwood—Kenwood: a Devonshire Family, by Richard Gresly, 1978.

Kildare, Earls of—The Earls of Kildare, and their Ancestors: from 1057 to 1773, by the Marquis of Kildare, Second Edition, 1858. Addenda, 1862, 2 vols, Dublin, 1858-62.

King—The Kings, Earls of Kingston, Cambridge, 1959.*

Kingdon—The Kingdon Family, by F.B. Kingdon, 1974. A Second Look, by A.S. Kingdon, 1974.

Knatchbull-Hugessen—A Kentish Family, by Sir H.M. Knatchbull-Hugesson, 1960.

Knapp—An Account of the Knapp Family of Gloucestershire, by R.F. Moody, 1964.*

Knight—A Brief History of the Knight Family, by P. Beesley, 1964.

Knightley—Seemmata et Propogationes Antiquae Familiae de Knightley, copied from the original roll in the possession of Sir R. Knightley of Fawsley, 4to, 1867 (25).*

L

Langley—The Langley Family and Its Cartulary, by Peter R. Coss, Dugdale Society, 1974.

Larcom—History of the Families of Larcom, Hollis and McKinley, by M. Burrows, Oxford, 1883.*

Lauder—Notes on Historical References to the Scottish Family of Lauder, edited by James Young, 4to, Glasgow, 1884.

Lawrence—The Lawrences, by Nathaniel Harris, illustrated by Andrew Farmer, London, 1976.

Lee—Related to Lee, by R.H.M. Lee, 1963-5.

Lehmann—Ancestors and Friends, by J. Lehmann, 1962.

Leith-Hay—Trustie to the End: the Story of the Leith Hall Family, by H. Leith Hay and M. Lochhead, 1957.

Livingstone—The Livingstone Family in America and Its Scottish Origins, by F. van Rensselaer, 1949.

Lloyd—Fruitful Heritage, by E. Allison, 1952.
  J. Bevan Braithwaite: a Friend of the Nineteenth Century, 1909.
  Records of a Clerical Family, by H.S. Eeles, 1959.

Lockhart—Seven Centuries: a History of the Lockharts of Lee and Carnwath, by Simon Macdonald Lockhart, Carnwath, 1977.*

Loffroy—The Loffroy of Cambray, by J.A.P. Loffroy, 1961.

Lofts—Roots and Branches: A Family History of Lofts, Newling,

Wisb(e)y and Associated Families of Cambridgeshire and Essex, compiled by Margaret Pitt, London, 1979.

Longridge—Genealogical Notes of the Kindred Families of Longridge, Fletcher, and Hawks, collected and arranged by R.E.C. Waters, [1871].*

Lougher—The Loughers of Glamorgan, by J. Lougher, Cardiff, 1952.

Lumley—A North-Country Estate: the Lumleys and Saundersons, by T.W. Beastall, 1974.
Family Lineage and Civil Society, by M. James, n.d.

Lyttleton—The Lyttletons, a Family Chronicle, by Betty Askwith, London, 1975.
From Peace to War, by O. Lyttelton, 1968.

M

MacAulay—Poets and Historians, by M. Mooreman, 1974.

McCann—Origin of the McCanns, by A. Matthews, 1973.

McDonnell—The Antrim McDonnells, by A. Antrim, 1979.

MacHenry—The Family of MacHenry of New South Wales, by C.E. Lugard, 1947.

MacDonnell—The MacDonnells of Antrim, by M. Walsh, 1960.

MacDougall—A Short History of the Clan MacDougall, [by] Michael Starforth, [Oban], 1977.*

Mackay—The Clan Mackay, by R.L. Mackay, Third Edition, [Wolverhampton, 1978].*

MacKenzie—Some Mackenzie Pedigrees, by D. Warrand, 1965.

McKinley—See Larcom.

Mackintosh—The Mackintoshes and Clan Chattan, by A.M. Mackintosh, Edinburgh, 1903.*

Maclaren—The MacLarens: a History of the Clan Lashran, by M. MacLaren, Second Edition, 1978.

MacLean—The Clan Maclean, by J. Mackechmie, 1954.

MacLennan—History of the MacLennans, 1978.

McLeod—The Broad Canvas: a History of My Mother's Family, by Lolita Jean Cameron, Chesham, 1974.

McNair—McNair, McNear and McNeir Genealogies, by J.B. McNair, Chicago, 1923.*

MacPherson—The Macphersons and Magees, by L. Macpherson Crawford, 1949.

MacRory—The Past MacRorys of Duneane, Castle-Dawson, Limavady and Belfast, by R.A. MacRory, n.d.

MacSweeney—The Sween Clan of the Battle-Axe, by R.M. Sweeney, 1968.

Mainwaring—A Short History of Mainwaring Family, by R. Mainwaring Finley, London, 1976 (200). Facsimile reprint of the 1890 edition.

Mar—The Earldom of Mar in Sunshine and in Shade during 500 Years, by Alexander, Earl of Crawford and Balcarres, 2 vols, Edinburgh, 1882.

Mardall—The Family of Mardall of Wheathampstead, Some Notes and Records, by C. William, 1950.

Marsh—Some Notice of Various Families of the Name of Marsh, by G.E.C[okayne] , London, Pollard, 1900.

Marshall—A Pedigree of the Descendants of Isaac and Rebecca Marshall of Perlethorpe, Notts., 1868 (20).*
The Marshall Family of West Sussex and of Gloucestershire, Notes by Charles Wallace Marshall, Exeter, 1973.

Martin—Parsons and Prisons, by B.E. Martin, 1972.

Martineau—Pedigrees of the Martineau Family, by C. Anthony Crofton, Northampton, 1972.

Maskelyne—Basset Down: an Old Country House, by M. Arnold-Foster, 1950.

Mason—A Note on Charles Mason's Ancestry, by H.W. Robinson, 1949.

Maugham—Somerset and All the Maughams, by Robin Maugham, London, 1975.

Mawle—The Mawle Family of South Northamptonshire and North Oxfordshire, compiled by Barbara Adkins, Banbury, 1969.

Maxse—The Maxse Paper, by F.W. Steer, 1964.

Maxwell—Annals of One Branch of the Maxwell Family, by Sir W.G. Maxwell, 1959.

Mayell—In Search of Ancestors, by F.L. Meyell, London, 1975.

Maylam—Maylam Family Records, First Series, by P. Maylam, 1932.

Meades—The Meades of Meaghstown Castle, by J.A. Meade, Victoria, B.C., 1953.
The Meades of Innishannon, 1956.

Mearns—See Angus.

Menhinick—A Monster at the Top of the Tree, by Kathleen Menhinick Dewey, London, 1975.

Menteith—The Red Book of Menteith, by Sir William Fraser, 2 vols, 4to, Edinburgh, 1880.

Merry—A Merry Family Omnibus, by Dorothy T. Merry, Shrewsbury, 1974 (50).*

Merryweather—Some Notes on the Family of Merryweather of England and America, by E.A. Merryweather, 1958.

Micklem—A History of the Micklem Family, by Ralph Micklem, 4to, Stanmore, 1954.*

Milhous—West with the Milhous and Nixon Families, by R.M. Bell, 1954.

Mitford—The Mitford Archives, by F.W. Steer, 1970.

Money-Kyrle—Some Records of the Money-Kyrle and Collateral Families, by B.E. Money, 1970.*

Montague—The Way of the Montagues, by B. Falk, n.d.

Moon—Yeoman, Craftsmen, Merchants: the Moons of Amondernes and Leylandshire, by R.C. Shaw, 1963.

Moorehouse—The Moorhouses of Bear Creek, by E.G. Moorehouse, Kingston, Canada, 1962.

Morgan—Cwrt-y-Gollen and its Families, by A.R. Hawkins, 1967.
    The House of Morgan, by E.P. Hoyt, 1968.

Morley—Heirs without Titles, by H.E.C. Stapleton, 1975.
    Some Morleys of South West Lancashire: a Genealogy, by
        Kenneth C. Morley, Bootle, 1978.

Morrell—Three Generations, by A. Vernon, 1966.

Moulton—See Foster.

Mountbatten—Manifest Destiny: a Study in Five Profiles of the
        Rise and Influence of the Mountbatten Family, by B.
        Connell, 1953.
    The Mountbattens: from Battenberg to Windsor, [by] Douglas
        Liversidge, London, 1978.

Mountenay—The Mounteney Family: a Miscellany, compiled by
        R.H. Mounteney, [London] , 1977.*

Munro—The Munro Tree: the Munros of Foulis and Other
        Families of the Clan: a Manuscript compiled in 1734, edited
        by R.W. Munro, Edinburgh, 1978.

Muriel—A Fenland Family: Some Notes on the History of a
        Family Surnamed Muriel . . . by J.H.L. Muriel, Ipswich,
        1977.

N

Napier—Revolution and the Napier Brothers, 1820-40, by Priscilla
        Napier, London, 1973.
    A Napier Background 1500-1974: an Account of the Napiers
        of Luton Hoo (1600-1747) and of the Descendants of the
        Branch which Settled in Woodstock . . . Ireland . . . by Sir
        Joseph W.L. Napier Bt., 1974.*

A Difficult Country: the Napiers of Scotland, by P. Napier, 1972.

Nelson—The Nelsons: the Family of Horatio Nelson, [by] Nathaniel Harris, illustrated by Andrew Farmer, London, 1977.

Newling—See Lofts.

Newton—A Record of Our Newton Family, by A.A. West, 1896.

Nixon—See Milhous.

Norrington—A Preliminary Account of the Norrington Family in Kent from the 13th to the 19th Century, compiled by John and Jeanette Norrington, Epsom, 1969.*

O

Oakeley—Some Links with the Past, by E.M. Oakeley, 1900.

Oakes—See Ray.

O'Brien—History of the Name O'Brien, [by] J.D. Williams, Dublin, 1977.

O'Byrne—The Book of the O'Byrnes, by E.O. Tuathail, n.d.

O'Doherty—Origin and History of the O'Dohertys, by Anthony Mathews, London, 1973.*

O'Donoghue—Origin and History of the O'Donoghues, by A. Matthews, 1973.

Oglander—Nunwell Symphony, by C. Aspinall-Oglander, 1945.

O'Kelly—History of the Name O'Kelly, [by] J.D. Williams,

Dublin, 1977.

O'Neill—History of the Name O'Neill, [by] J.D. Williams, Dublin, 1978.

Origin of the O'Neills with a History of the Septs, by Anthony Mathews, 1971.

Openshaw—The Openshaw Pedigree together with a Portion of the Ormerod Pedigree . . . by J.T. Openshaw, oblong folio, Bury, 1893.

Ormerod—See Openshaw, Thursby.

Orrery—The Orrery Papers, edited by the Countess of Cork and Orrery, 2 vols, 1903.

O'Sullivan—History of the Name O'Sullivan, [by] J.D. Williams, Dublin, 1978.

Oxx—The Oxx Family, by W.G. Oxx, California, 1975.

P

Palgrave—Palgrave Family Memorials, edited by C.J. Palmer and S. Tucker, Norwich, 1878.*

The Palgraves of Rollesby, a Brief History, 1773-1973, by Derek A. Palgrave, Doncaster, 1973.*

Archives of Flegg, relating to the Palgraves [by Derek A. Palgrave], Doncaster, 1975.

The Palgraves of Ludham, by Patrick T.R. Palgrave-Moor, Doncaster, 1977.

The History and Lineage of the Palgraves, [by] Derek A. Palgrave, Doncaster, 1978.

Palmer—The Palmers of Dorney Court, by T.W.E. Roche, 1971.

Panter—The Seed is for Sowing, by A.E. Panter, 1972.

Parker—The Parkers at Saltram, by R. Fletcher, 1970.

Paston—The Pastons: the Story of a Norfolk Family, Norwich
      Castle Museum, 1953.
   The Pastons 1378-1732, by K.N. Marshall, 1956.
   The Pastons and Their England, by H.S. Bennet, 1968.

Pattle—Julia Margaret Cameron: A Victorian Portrait, by B. Hill,
      1973.

Peak—The Peak-Peake Family History, by C.H. Peake and C.J.
      Snow, California, 1975.
   The History of the Peake Family of Denbighshire, Wales, London
      and New Zealand, by A.G. Peake, 1975.*

Pelham—The Rise of the Pelhams, by J.B. Owen, 1957.

Pell—Pelliana. Pell of Pelham, by T. Pell, New York, 1962.

Pennington—Penningtonia. Pedigree of Sir Josslyn Pennington, 5th
      baron Muncaster . . . by Joseph Foster, 4to, 1878.

Pepys—The Descendants of John Pepys, by J.S. Gordon Clark,
      1964.

Percy—A Sketch of the Male Descendants of Josceline de
      Louvaine, the Second House of Percy, Earls of Northumber-
      land . . . by W.E. Surtees, Newcastle-on-Tyne, 1844.

Piper—Sir Hugh Piper the Knighted Hero of Launceston and his
      Descendants, by O.B. Peter, n.d.

Poingdestre—Poingdestre-Poindexter: A Norman Family Through
      the Ages, 1250-1977, by J.P. Landers and R.D. Poindexter,

Austin, Texas, 1977.

Pole—The Story of Shute: the Bonvilles and the Poles, by M.F. Bridie, Axminster, 1955.

Pollock—The Pollock Pedigree 1080-1950, by A. Pollock and E.A. Langslow Cox, 1950.

Pomeroy—History and Genealogy of the Pomeroy Family, by W. Pomeroy, U.S.A., 1958.

Pontifex—The Family of Pontifex of West Wycombe, Co. Buckingham, 1500-1977, by Claud E.C. Pontifex, [Hassocks], 1977* (200).

Poole—The Pooles of County Cork, by R. ffolliott, 1956.

Popham—A West Country Family: The Pophams from 1150, by Frederick W. Popham, Sevenoaks, 1976.* (250).

Potter—From Ploughshare to Parliament: a Short Memoir of the Potters of Tadcaster, by G. Meineetzhagen, 1908.

Powell—Pedigree of the Family of Powell, sometime resident at Mildenhall, Barton Mills . . . Suffolk, afterwards at Homerton and Clapton . . . by E. Powell, 4to, 1891.*

Power—Notes and Pedigrees Relating to the Family of Poher, Poer, or Power, by Edmund 17th Lord Power, n.d.

Prescott—The Chronicles of the Prescotts of Ayrfield, Co. Lancaster, by E.P. Hill and C.P. Prescot, 1937.*

Price—The Descendants of Alfred Hervey Price, by Q. Nelson, 1973.

Puget—The Puget Family in England, by Percy G. Dawson, 1976*
(40).

Puleston—The Early Pulestons, by Sunter Harrison, Wrexham,
1975.*

Pyne—The James, Pyne, Dixon Family Book, compiled by Alicia
C. Percival, 1977.

Q

Quisenbury—Memories of the Quisenbury Family in Germany,
England and America, by A.C. Quisenberry, Washington,
1900.

R

Radcliffe, Radclyffe—Pedigree of Radclyffe. From Register of
Pedigrees 'Norfolk 2' in the College of Arms, 4to, 1876.
Wrenche (Pransiaid) and Radcliffe: Notes on Two Families of
Glamorgan, by W.G. Wrenche, 1956.

Raikes—Pedigree of Raikes, by R.D. Raikes, Chichester, 1975;
1980.

Rank—The Master Millers: the Story of the House of Rank,
Joseph Rank Ltd, 1955.

Rawlins—Family Quartette. [Rawlins, Hooper, Windham and
Russell], by C.W.H. Rawlins, Yeovil, 1962.*

Rawlinson—The Rawlinsons of Furness, compiled by Lynette
Cunliffe, Ulverston, 1978.
See also Ray.

Ray—Pedigree of Ray of Denston, Wickhambrook and Other

Places in Suffolk [with Oakes, Rawlinson, Heigham and Hasted], by G. Milner-Gibson-Cullum, 1903* (100).

Redman—The Redmans of Halfway House: the Story of a Wiltshire Family, by Clodagh O'Grady, Ramsbury, 1978.

Reeves—Sheepbell and Ploughshare: the Story of Two Village Families [Reeves and Whitaker], [by] Marjorie Reeves, Bradford-on-Avon, 1975.

Retallick—Retallick *et aliorum*, compiled by A.V. Retallick, 1979,

Ridge—A Sussex Family: the Family of Ridge Since 1500 to the Present Day, by Dudley Ridge, London, 1975.

Rigall—The Family of Riggall-Rigaud, by R.M. Riggall, 1963.

Roberts—Robert Roberts and his Family, by Brian Slyfield, Sussex, 1974.
A Brief Record of Our Family, by E.T. Roberts, 1952.

Roper—The Roper Family, 1960.

Rose—Roses Revisited, by J.A. Nunamaker, 1963.
The Rose Family, Part I, by G.C.B. Poulter, 1954.

Ross—Family Tree, by Mary Race, Ilfracombe, 1977.

Rothschild—The Rothschilds, a Family of Fortune, by Virginia Cowles, 1973, 1975.
The Rothschilds at Waddesdon Manor, by Mrs James de Rothschild, 1979.
The Rothschilds: a Family Portrait, by F. Morton, 1962, 1964.
The Romance of the Rothschilds, by I. Balla, 1913.

Routh—A Short History of the Family of Routh, by H.C. Edric Routh, 1953.

Rowallon—Historie and Descent of the House of Rowallane. Written in or prior to 1657 by Sir William Mure, Glasgow, 1825.

Russell—Woburn and the Russells, by G.S. Thomson, 1956. See also Rawlins.

Rutherford—Genealogical History of the Rutherford Family, compiled by W.K. Rutherford and A.C. (Zimmerman) Rutherford, Revised Edition, 2 vols, U.S.A., 1979.

S

Sabin, Sabine—Origin and Development of the Surname Sabin, by W.H.W. Sabine, n.d.
Sabin(e), The History of an Ancient English Surname, New York, Colburn and Tegg, 1953.

Saddington—Some Saddington Families, by S.W. Saddington, Woking, 1977.

Sage—History of the Sage and Slocum Families of England and America . . . by the Hon. R. and M.O. Sage, 4to, New York, 1908.

St. Aubyn—The St. Aubyns of Cornwall, 1200-1977, by Diana Hartley, Chesham, 1977.

Salomons—David Salomons House, by M.D. Brown, 1968.

Samuel—The Samuel Family of Liverpool and London from 1755 onwards, by R.J.D'A. Hart, 1958.

Sanxay–The Sanxay Family, by T.F. Sanxay, New York, 1907.

Sassoon–The Sassoons, by S. Jackson, 1968.

Saunders–The Saunders, Sanders, Sandars Family and its Blood Connections, compiled by T. Homer-Saunders, n.d.

Saunderson–See Lumley.

Savage–The Family of Savage of Co. Wilts, by L.G.H. Horton-Smith, 1944.

Savary–A Genealogical and Biographical Record of the Savery Families (Savory and Savary) and of the Severy Family . . . by A.W. Savary, Boston, U.S.A., 1893-1905.

Savill–Savills: a Family and a Firm 1652-1977, [by] John A.F. Watson, 1977.

Scarr–A History of the Scarr Family (circa 1581-1977), by J.R. Scarr, Second Edition, Oxford, 1977.*

Scott–The Scotts, by J.M. Scott, 1957.

Seaver–History of the Seaver Family, by G. Seaver, 1950.

Seckford–A Tudor Worthy, Thomas Seckford of Woodbridge, by A. Daly Briscoe, Foreword by Norman Scarfe, Ipswich, 1979.

Seymour–Ordeal by Ambition, by W. Seymour, 1972.

Shakespeare–The Shakespeares, by Nathanial Harris, London, 1976.

Sharman–The Roll Baronetcy and Certain Sharman Families, by

G.A. Sharman, 1972.

Shaw—The Shaws: the Family of George Bernard Shaw, [by] Nathaniel Harris, illustrated by Andrew Farmer, London, 1977.

Shuttleworth—Backcloth to Gawthorpe, by Michael P. Conroy, London, 1971.

Sidney—The Pedigree of Sir Philip Sidney, compiled by R. Cooke, 1869.*

Skilbeck—The Skilbecks: Dry Salters 1650-1950, by D. Dawe, 1950.

Slocum—See Sage.

Smith—A Family of Friends, by R.A. Parker, 1960.

Smyth—The Rise of a Gentry Family: the Smyths of Ashton Court 1500-1642, by J.H. Bettey, Bristol, 1978.
The Inside Story of the Smyths of Ashton Court, by Anton Bantock, Bristol, 1977.

Smythe—Pedigree of Smythe of Ortenhanger, of Smythe of Bidborough and Sutton at Hone, by John J. Stocker, 1892.

Sneyd—The Sneyds and Keele Hall, by J.M. Kolbert, 1967, Keele, 1976.
Versicles and Hoardings, by F.M. Doherty, 1968.

Sorley—Sorley Pedigree, by Col. Merrow Sorley, folio, 1965.*

Sowerby—The Sowerby Saga, by A. de C. Sowerby, 1952.

Sparling—Pages from the Life of John Sparling of Petton, edited

by his daughter who has added accounts of the families of
Trafford, Cunliffe, etc., 4to, 1904.*

Spencer—A Short History of Althorp and the Spencer Family,
1949.

Spilhaus—Arnold William Spilhaus, Reminiscences and Family
Records, edited by M.W. Spilhaus, 1950.

Stacy—Simon Stacy and his Descendants, by Virginia (Meadows)
McCann, U.S.A., 1978.

Stafford—The Staffords, Earls of Stafford and Dukes of Buckingham 1394-1521, [by] Carol Rawcliffe, Cambridge U.P.,
1978.

Standish—The Standish Family, by E. Johnson, 1972.

Stanhope—Annals of a Yorkshire House, by A.M.W. Stirling, 2 vols,
1911.

Stevens—Ancestry of Col. John Harrington Stevens and his Wife
Helen Miller, by M.L. Holman, 1948.

Stewart, Stuart—An Essay on the Origine of the Royal Family of
Stewarts in Answer to Dr. Kennedy's . . . Dissertation by
Richard Hay, sm. 4to, Edinburgh, 1722.
The Stewarts, by J. Stewart, 1955.

Stonor—Stonor: A Catholic Sanctuary in the Chilterns, by R.J.
Stonor, 1951.

Strachey—The Strachey Family 1588-1932, by C.R. Sanders, 1953.
Two Victorian Families, by B. Askwith, 1971.

Strange—The Stranges of Tunbridge Wells, by C.H. Strange, 1948.

Strother—The Strother Family Notebook, compiled by A.P. Strother, jr., U.S.A., n.d.

Stuckey—Stuckeys of Somerset, by M. Churchman, Englewood, Colorado, 1966.

Studdert—The Studdert Family, by R.H. Studdert, 1960.

Sturgis—Child of Turgis: an Account of the Sturges-Turgis Family of Dorset, by G.W. Sturges, Clacton-on-Sea, 1978.

Styring—The Royal Heirs of Canute and South Yorkshire, by H.K. Styring, 1961.

Stubbs—A Royal Descent, with Other Pedigrees and Memorials [of the Stubbs family, of Beckbury Hall, Salop], by T.E. Sharpe, 1875 (100).*
Additions and corrections, 1881 (40).*
Additions and corrections, Part II, 1881 (40).*

Sutcliffe—The Family History of Helen, Barbara and Elizabeth Sutcliffe, compiled by Barry P. Sutcliffe, High Wycombe, 1976.

Sutherland—A Genealogical History of the Earldom of Sutherland from its Origin to 1630, continued to 1651 by Sir Robert Gordon, folio, Edinbrugh, 1813.

Swinnerton—The Swinnerton Family History, by I.S. Swinnerton, 1974.

Symonds—Ancestors and Descendants of John Symonds and Martha Florinda Ratsey of West Cowes, Isle of Wight, by O.E. Wallin, 1954.

Sykes—The Visitors' Book, [by] Christopher Simon Sykes,

London, 1978.

Synan—The Synan Family, by J.A. Gaughan, 1972.

T

Tangye—Some Notes on the Tangye Family, by J.F. Parker, 1972.

Tattersall—The Tattersalls, by V. Orchard, 1953.

Taylor—Pedigrees of the Family of Finch Taylor, edited by J. Philpot, 1872.

Tennant—The Tennants Stalk, by N. Crathorne, 1973.

Tennyson—The Tennysons, background to Genius, by Charles Tennyson and Hope Dyson, London, 1974.

Thayer—The Thayer Family of Brockworth, by L.T. Ojeda, 1947.

Theobald—Pedigree of the Theobalds of Kent, by Mrs Theodore Stephenson, 1913.

Thomas—The Thomas Family of Zennor, Cornwall, by G.J. Anderson, n.d.

Thrale—A New Thraliana: a Chronicle of the Thrale Family of Hertfordshire, by Richard Thrale, St. Albans, 1973.*

Thornhill—The Dispossessed, by B. Kerr, 1974.

Thursby—Some Notes on the Families of Thursby of Abington, Hargreaves of Ormerod House, and Thursby of Ormerod House, by W.A.L., 1908.

Tidey—The Tideys of Washington, Sussex, 1773-1973, by Merle

Tidey, Bala, Wales, [1973].

Tillinghast—The Tillinghast Family, by R.C. Tillinghast, Washington, U.S.A., 1973.

Tottenham—The Family of Tottenham, by Sir R. Tottenham, 1960.

Townely—The Towneleys of Towneley: a Chronicle of the Life and Times of the Later Towneleys, [by] Leslie Chapples, [Burnley], [1976].*

Trafford—See Sparling.

Tregenza—The Tregenza Family, by Paul Tregenza, 1975.
The Tregenza Family, by Paul Tregenza, Revised Edition, 1979.

Tregoning—Some Stalwart Cornish Emigrants, by E.M. Tregoning, 1963.

Trelawny—Trelawne and Bishop Trelawny, by W.H. Paynter, 1962.

Trevanion—See Byron.

Trevelyan—Poets and Historians, by M. Mooreman, 1974.

Turnbull—A Shipping Venture, by A. and R. Long, 1974.

Twenebrokes—Chapters Relating to the Family of Twenebrokes, by M.G. Glazebrook, Northampton, 1975.

Tyler—See Bradley.

Tyrrell—A Genealogical History of the Tyrrells, by Joseph Henry Tyrell, (1904), Reprint 1979 (100).

Genealogical Notes on the Tyrrell and Terrell Families, by
    E.H. Terrell, San Antonio, Texas, U.S.A., 1907.
Further Notes. Second edition, by E.H. Terrell, 1909.
The Tyrells of England, by Oliver F. Brown, Chichester, 1980.

V

Vansittart—Story of Bisham Abbey, by P. Compton, 1973.

Vaux—Vaux of Harrowden a Recusant Family, by G. Anstruther,
    1953.

Verey—The Verey Family, by A. Verey, Australia, 1968.

Villiers—A Villiers Genealogy, by R.G. Couzens, n.d.

W

Walcot—The Walcots of Birmingham and Bristol, by M.G. and
    P.J. Walcot, Sutton Coldfield, 1975* (100).

Wallace—Sagas of the Wallace Clan, by G.A. Wallis, 1978.

Walpole—One Generation of a Norfolk House. A Contribution to
    Elizabethan History, by Augustus Jessop, 1878, 1879 and
    1913.

Warburg—The Warburgs, by David Farrer, London, 1975.

Washbourne—Some Notes on the Evesham Branch of the Wash-
    bourne Family, by E.A.B. Barnard, Evesham, 1914.

Waters—The Waters or Walter Family of Cork, by C.W. Waters,
    1939.

Watts—Watts in a Name, by M.J. and C.T. Watts, [1975?].

Wedgwood—Uncommon People, by P. Bloomfield, 1955.
The Story of Wedgwood, by A. Kelly, 1975.

Wells—Swithun Wells and the Bambridge Story, by K.M. Downs, Eastleigh, Hants, 1979.*

Wentworth—The Wentworth Papers, by J.P. Cooper, 1973.

Whitaker—Princes under the Volcano, by Raleigh Trevelyan, 1972.
Sheep Bell and Ploughshare: the Story of Two Village Families [Reeves and Whitaker] [by] Marjorie Reeves, Bradford-on-Avon, 1978.

Whiting—Notes and Materials Towards a History of Whiting of Wood: a Mediaeval Family . . . by Richard Whiting, 1974.

Wiffen—Historical Memoirs of the First Race of Ancestry whence the House of Russell had its Origin, by J.H. Wiffen, 1833 (An Introduction to the 'Memoirs of the House of Russell, 2 vols, 1833).

Wilberforce—The Wilberforce Archives, by F.W. Steer, 1966.

Wilde—The Wildes of Merrion Square, by P. Byrne, 1953.

Wilder—The Wilder Family: The Wilders of Ipsden, Oxon, by W.C. Wilder, 1974.

Willis—Report on Research into the Ancestry of the Willis Family, by A.J. Willis, 1951.

Wilson—The Snuff Makers of Sheffield, by M.H.F. Chaytor, 1963.
The Fair Isle Wilsons, by Alan T. Wilson, 1973.
Descendants of Isaac and Rachel Wilson [Wilson of Kendal, Westmoreland], by R. Seymour Benson, revised by M.E. and

J.S. Benson, 1949* 4 vols.

Windham—Felbrigg: the Story of a House, by R.W. Ketton-Cremer, 1962.
See also Rawlins.

Winnington-Ingram—Short History of the Winnington-Ingram, by A.J. and E.J. Winnington-Ingram, 1968(?).

Winslow—The Winslows of Kempsey, by Lt. Cmdr. D.K. Winslow, 1953.
Mayflower Heritage: a Family Record, by D.K. Winslow, 1957.

Wisby, Wisbey—See Lofts.

Wood—See Cranmer.

Woodleigh—The Woodleighs of Amscote, by M. Collins and P. Cotton, 1885.

Woodruff—Memorials of the Family of Woodruff, by C.E. Woodruff, 4to, 1889.*

Woodward—Woodwards of the Forest of Galtres, by F.H. Woodward, 1970.

Wortley—Magic in the Distance: a Chronicle of Five Generations by Violet Stuart Wortley, 1948.

Wren—Wren Family History, 1776-1900; Dunmow, Lindsell and Thaxted, Essex, by Edna Gray, 1978.

Wrenche—See Radcliffe.

Wren—Wren Family: Lindsell/Great Dunmow/Thaxted, Essex, 1776-1900, compiled by Edna Grace Grey, Leigh-on-Sea, 1978.

Wright—Wright of Derby, by S.C. Kaines and H.C. Bemrose, 1922.

Wyatt—Cheyneys and Wyatts: a Brief History, by Sir S.C. Wyatt, 1960.

Wroth—Protestant Gentlemen: the Wroths of Dinants Arbour, Enfield and Loughton, Essex, by D.O. Pam, Enfield, 1973.

Wrottesley—History of the Family of Wrottesley of Wrottesley, by the Hon. G. Wrottesley, Exeter, 1903.

Wyly—Irish Origins, a Family Settlement in Australia, by D.A.A. Wyly, Tasmania, 1976 (750).

Wynch—Memoirs of the Wynch Family in India 1731-1914, by L.M. Wynch, n.d.

Yeamans—Yeamans, by G.S. Youmans, n.d.